HERE
Photographs by Graham Wilson

Here: Photographs by Graham Wilson

Copyright ©Graham Wilson
Printed in the United States of America.

Library and Archives Canada Cataloguing in Publication
Wilson, Graham, 1962-
    Here / Graham Wilson.
ISBN 978-1-927691-02-1

No part of this book may be reproduced, stored in a retrieval system, or transmitted in any form, by any means, without the prior permission of the publisher, except by a reviewer, who may quote brief passages in a review.

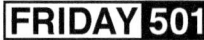

Box 31599, Whitehorse, Yukon, Canada, Y1A 6L2
www.friday501.com, info@friday501.com

There is a region south of Lima, Peru, that I visited in the spring of 2013. A highway divides a narrow strip between the mountains and the Pacific Ocean. Small communities and farms dot the arid landscape. At first glance it appears poor, weather-beaten, and endlessly fascinating in its subtleties.

When I quiet my mind, I'm surprised by my emotional response to place. Generally I prefer to travel slowly and wander alone. Perhaps it's the repetitiousness of walking that helps me relax and stop thinking "busy" thoughts. You hear the sound of a car engine sputter to start; a dog barks; rhythmic music pours from an open bedroom window. When you shake loose from thinking even an unfamiliar place is relatable. It's at these times that you feel awakened.

These photographs are abstractions with which I experimented with motion. My experience was unexpected and perhaps more emotional than it was intellectual. It was about taking an unfamiliar landscape and exploring what it feels like to experience a place for the first time. Here can be here, or here can be anywhere. When I revisited this region two months later and examined these photographs at the exact location they were taken, the images were familiar but the landscape seemed less exotic and I had an understanding that I did not have previously.
May 2013

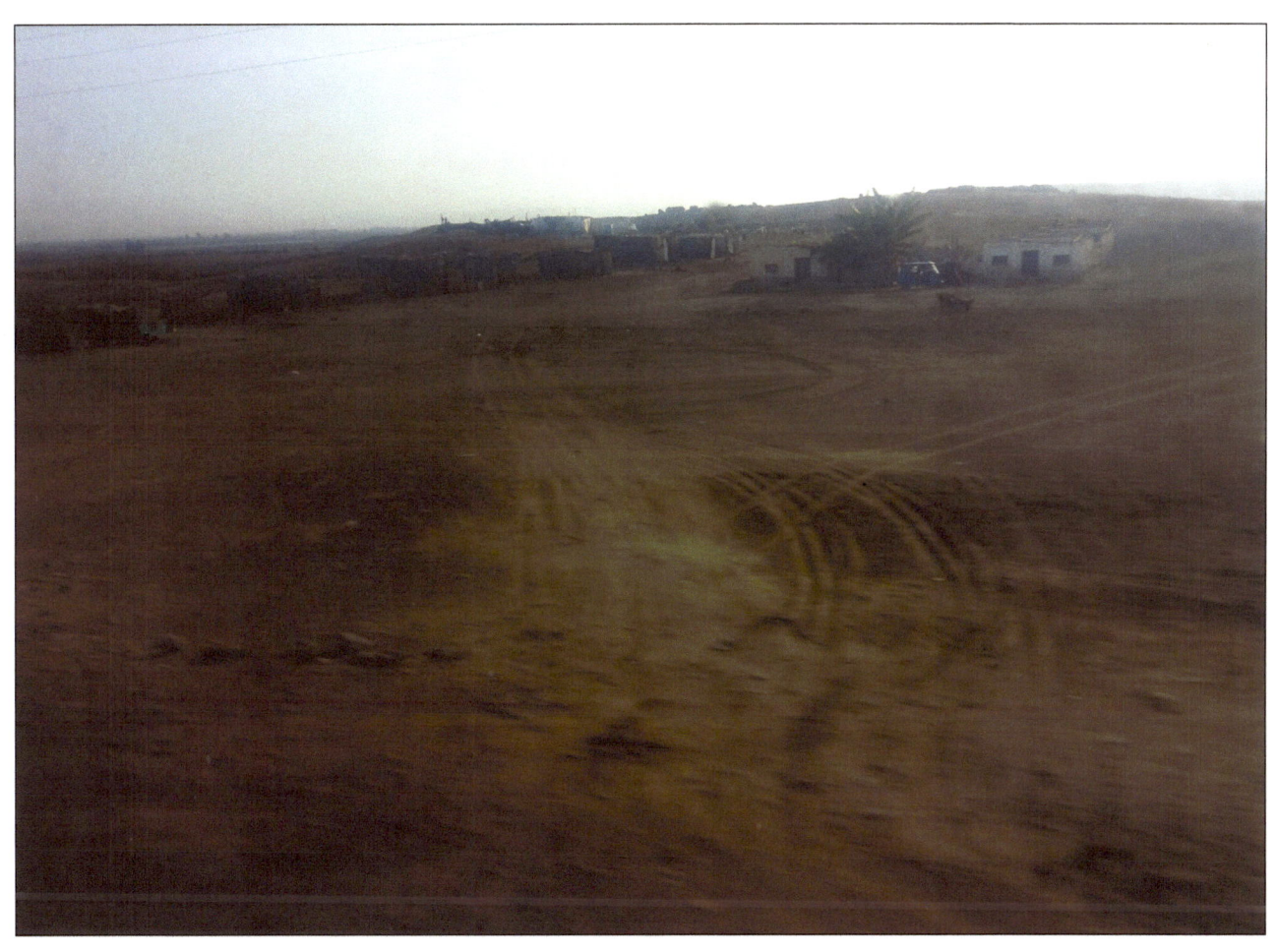

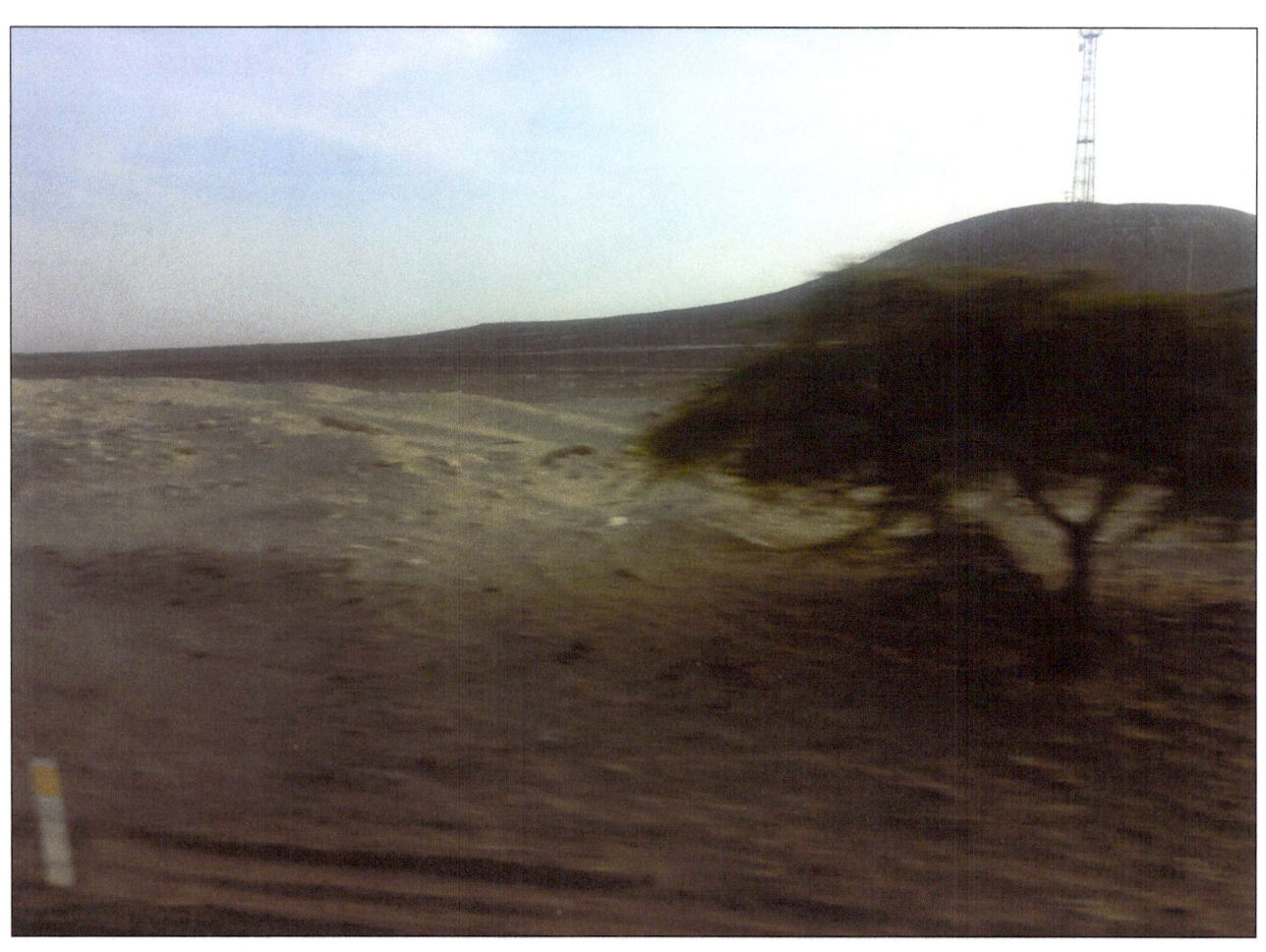

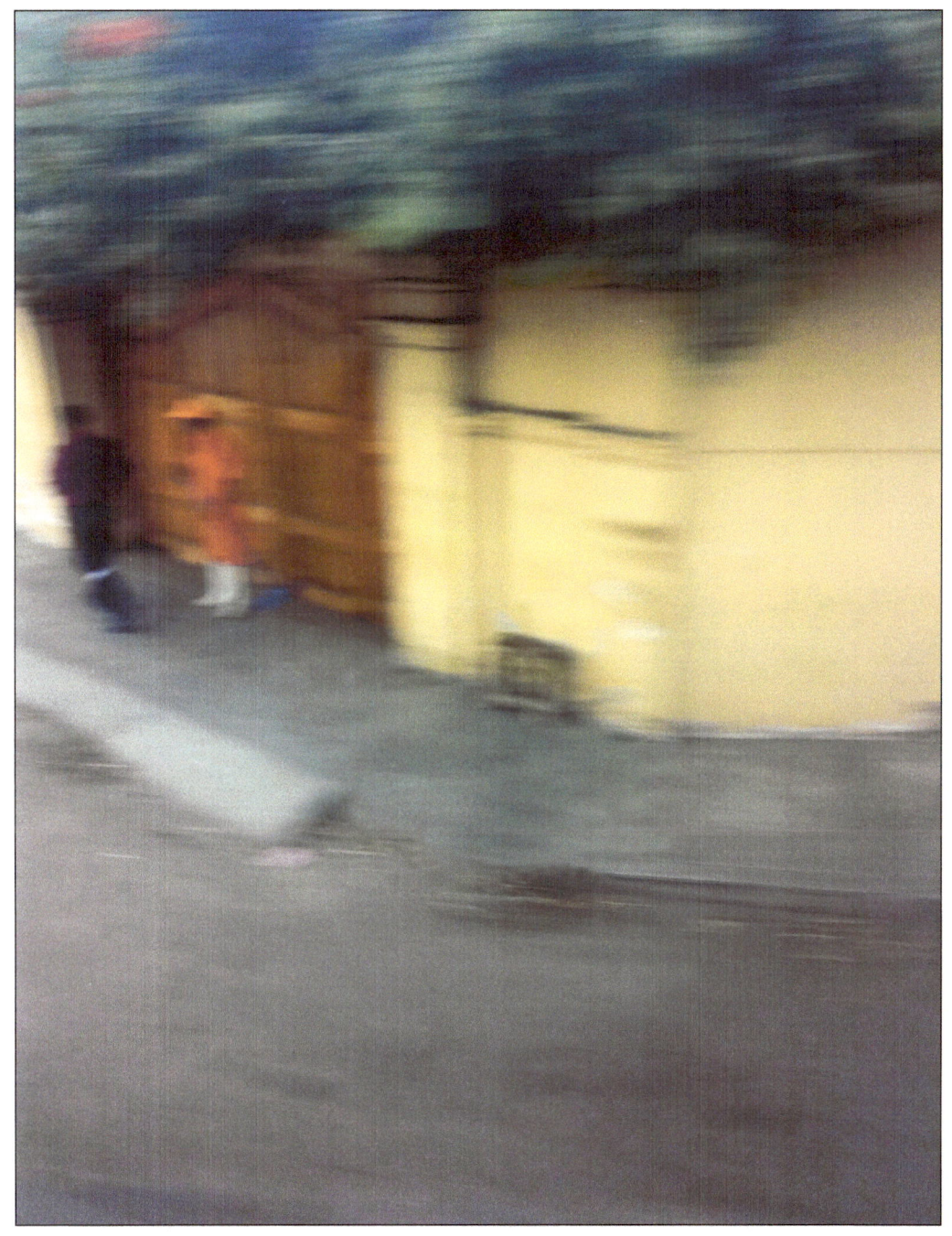

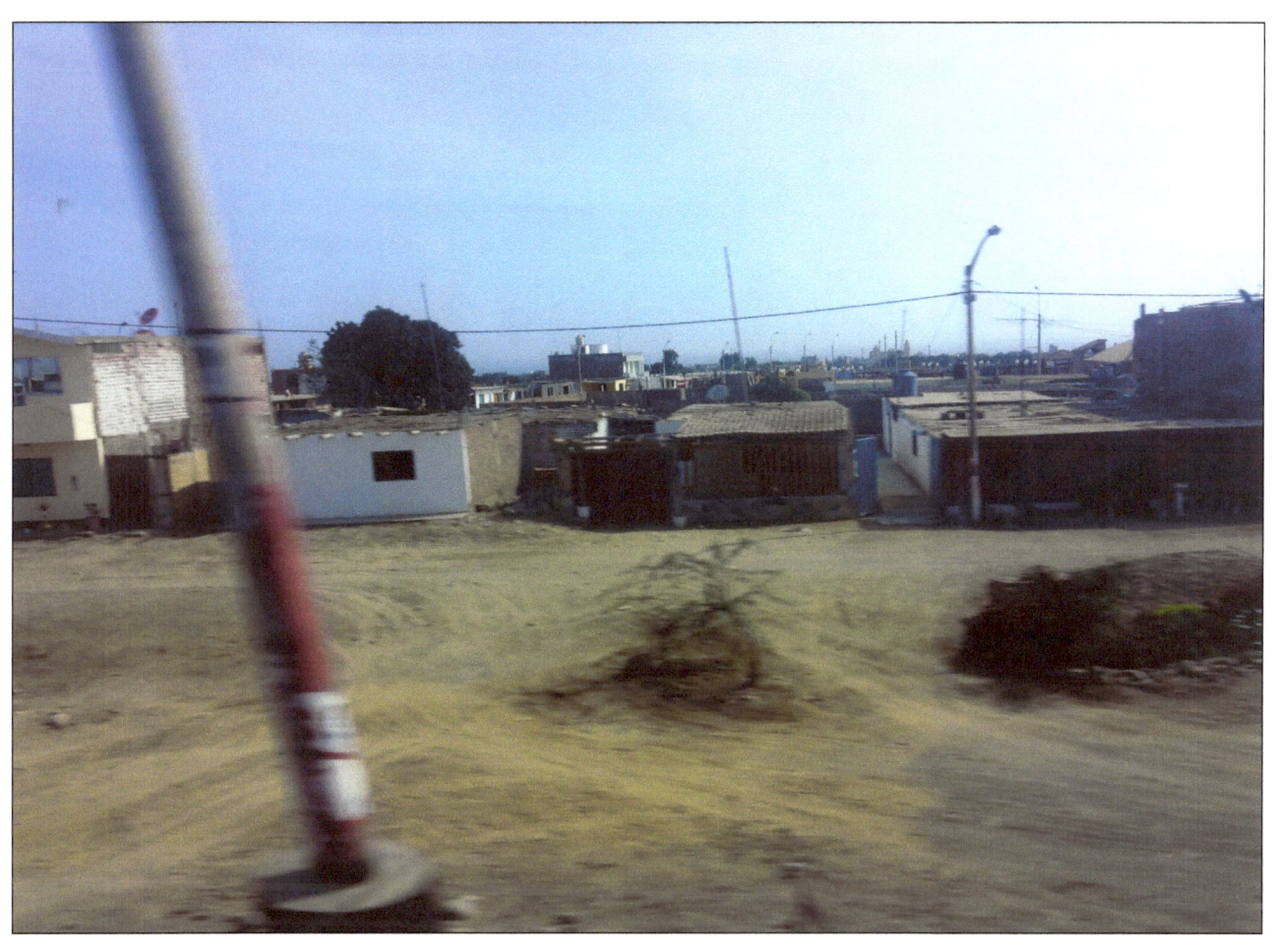

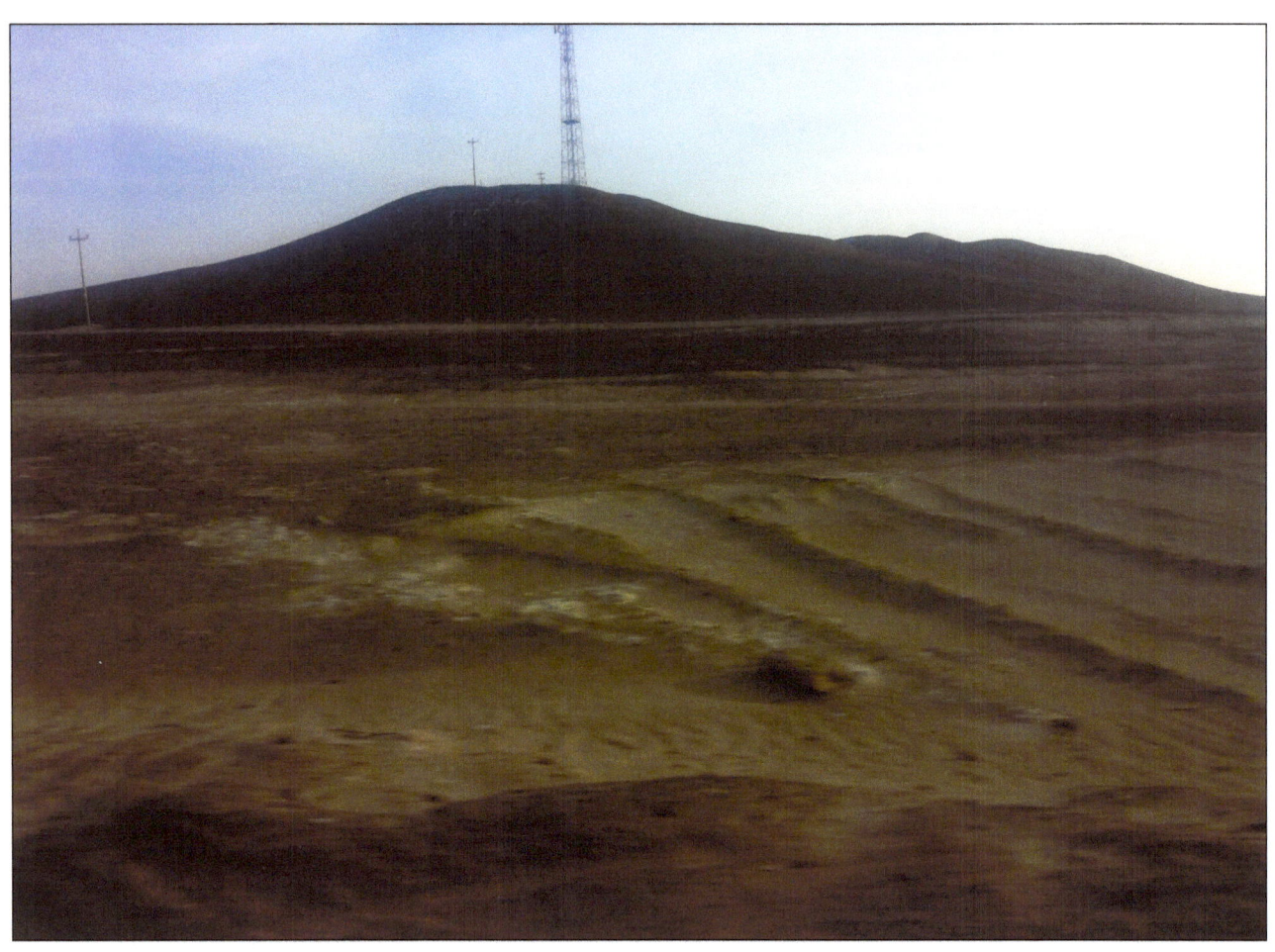

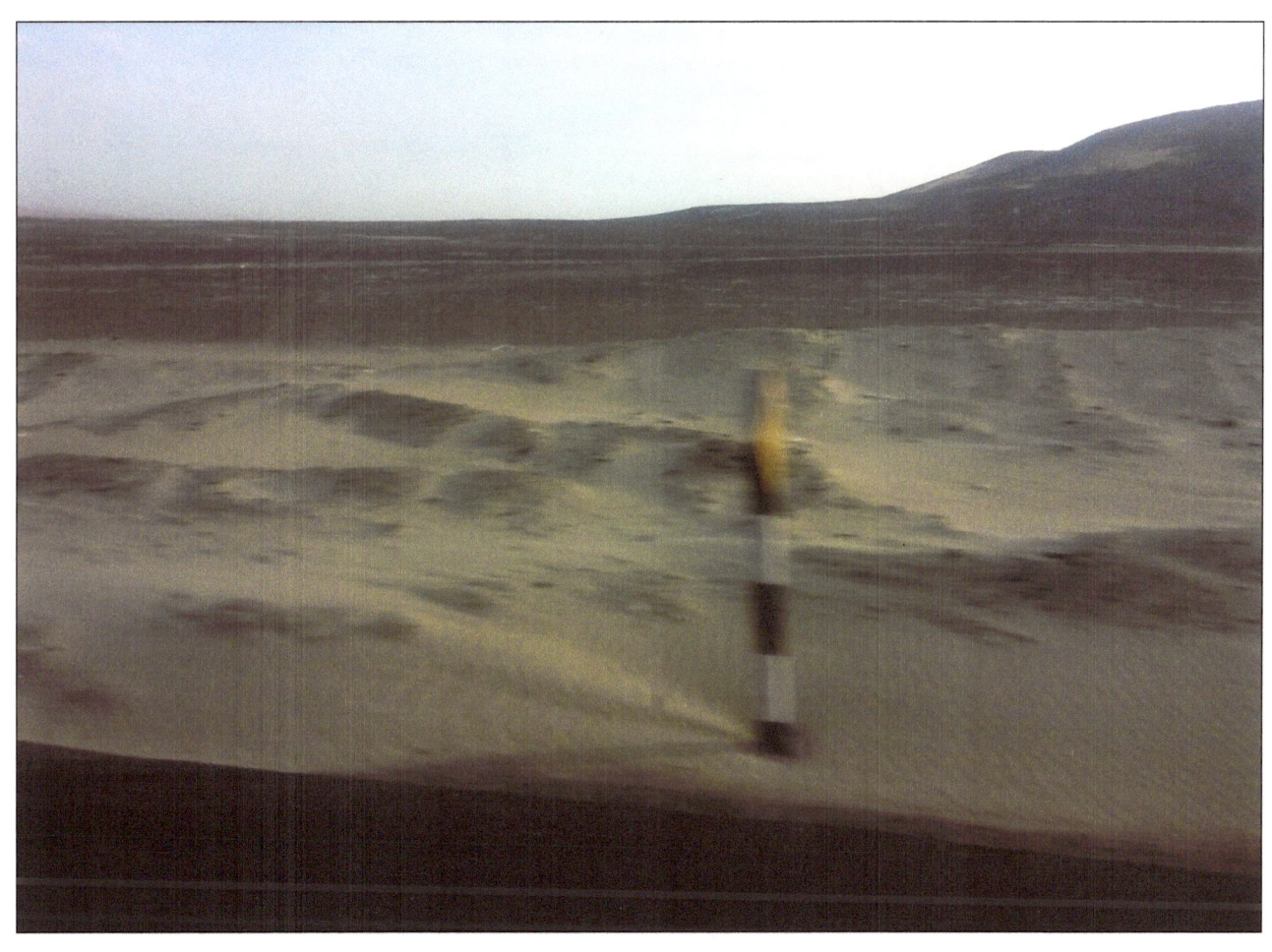

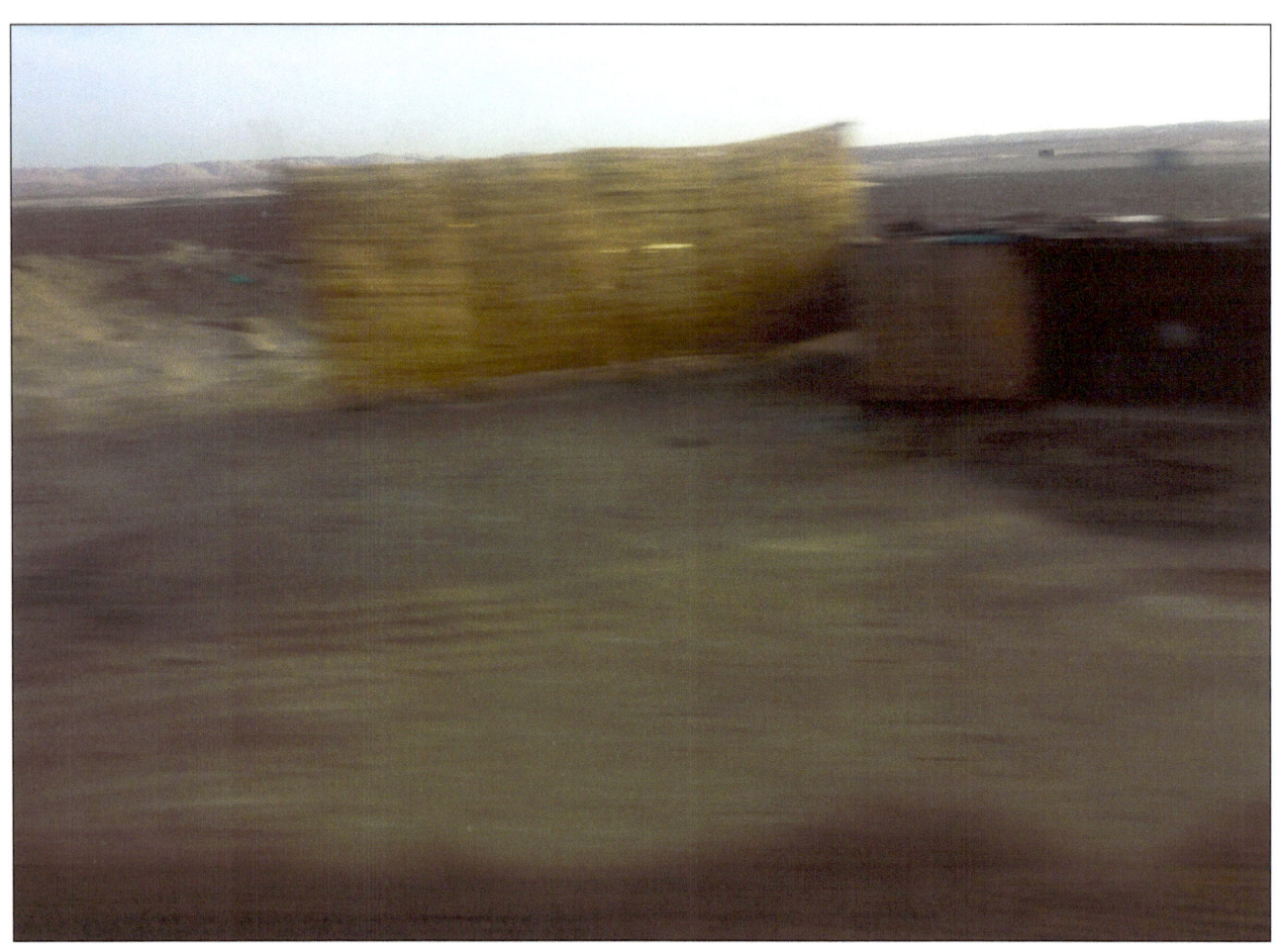

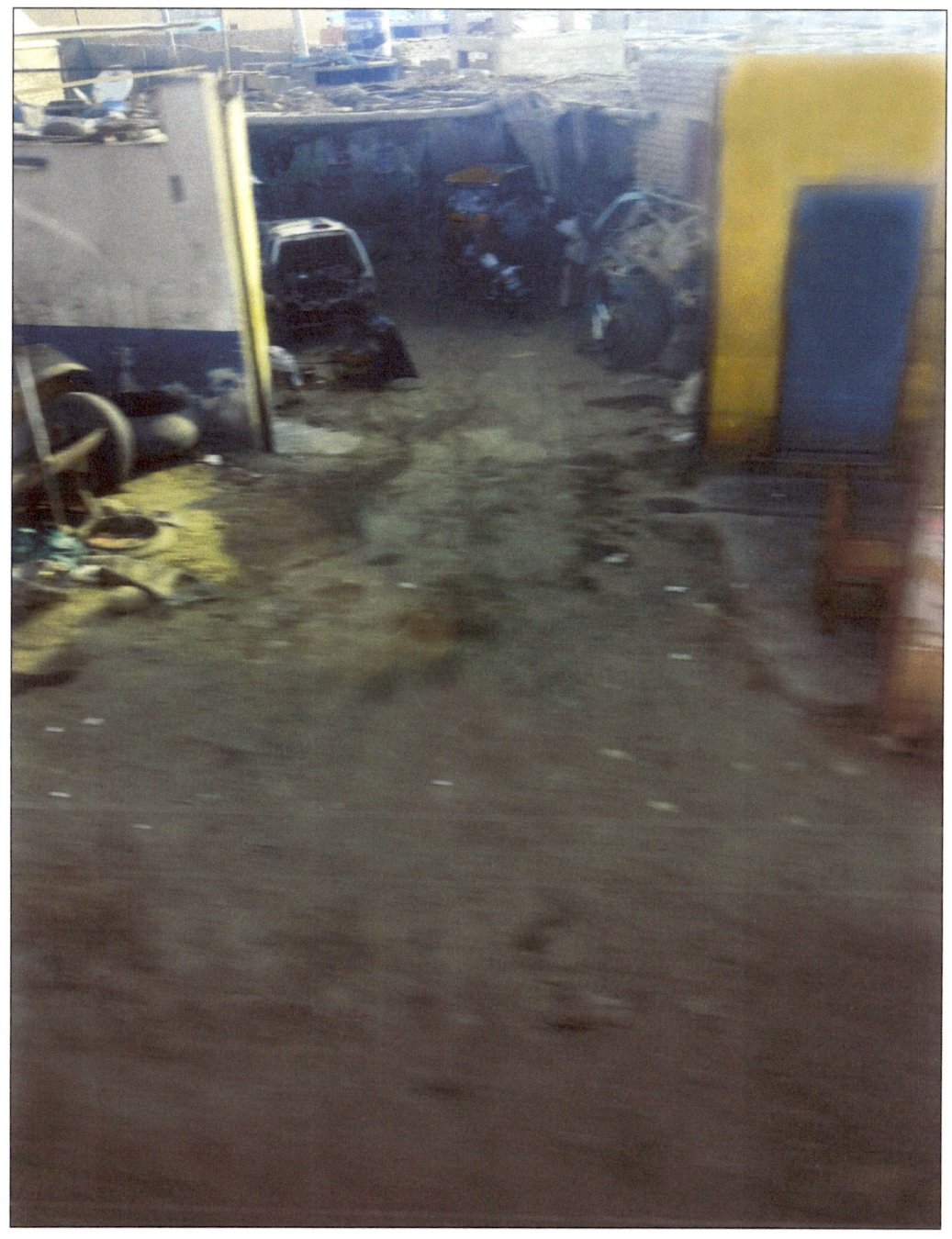

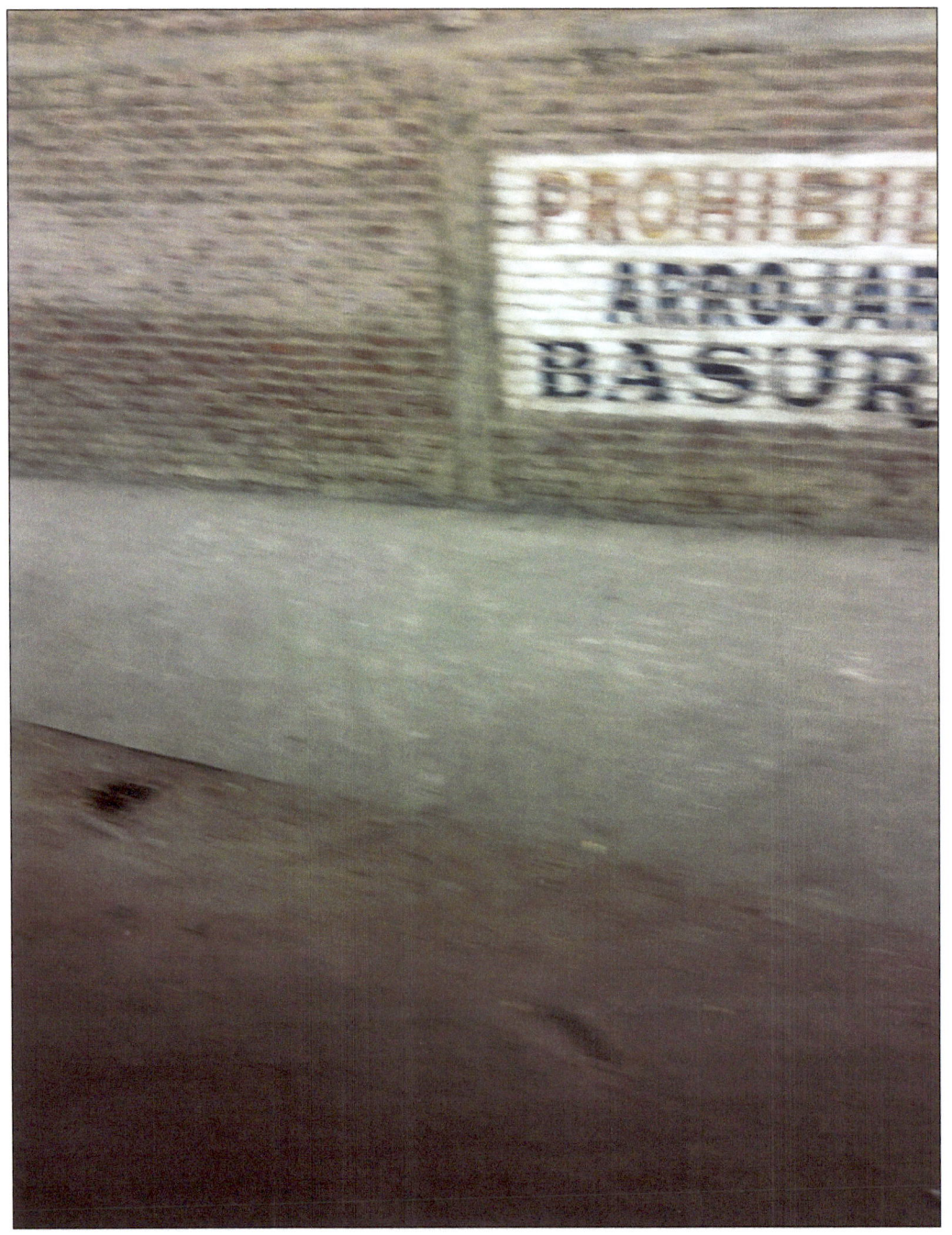

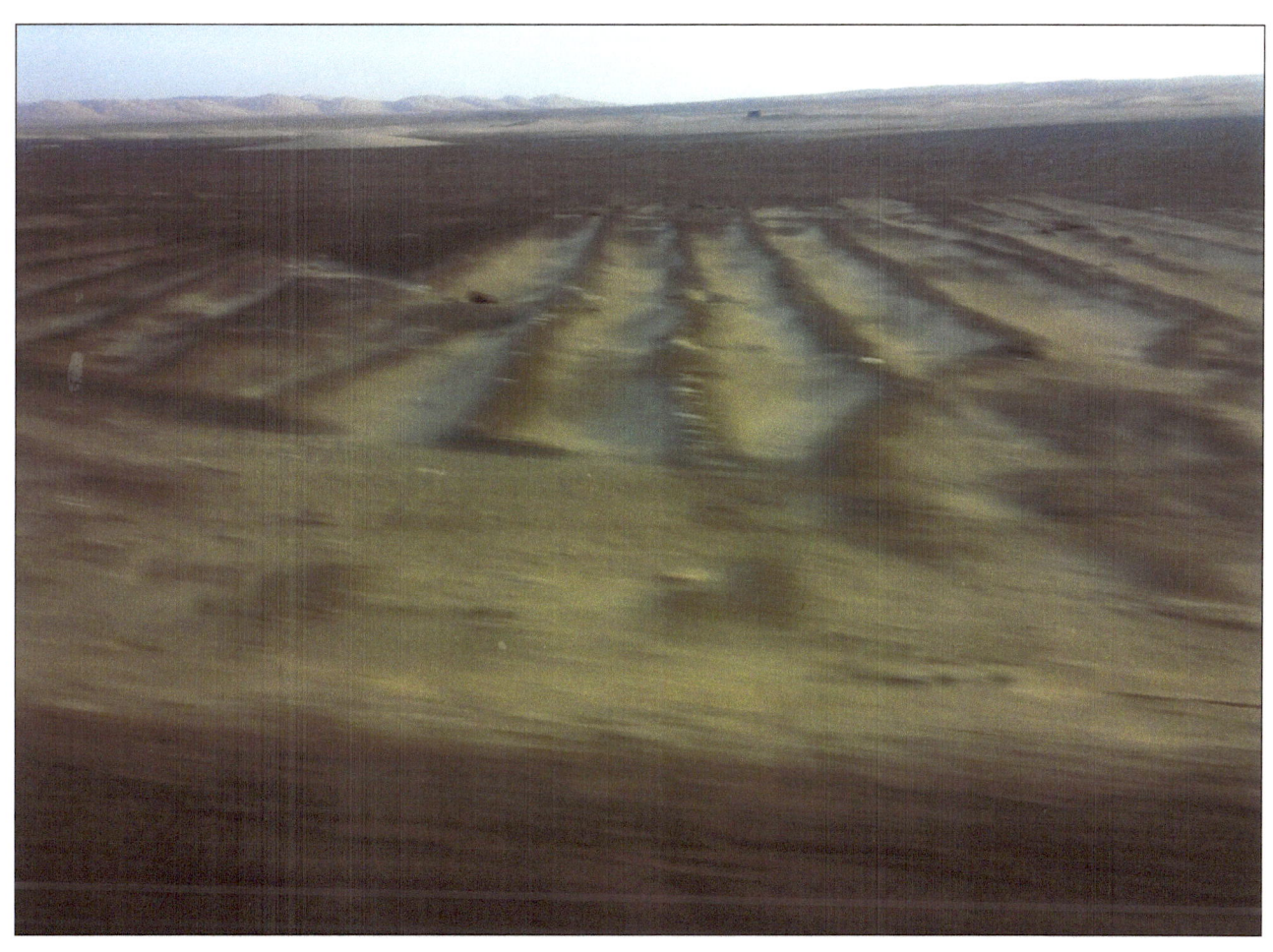

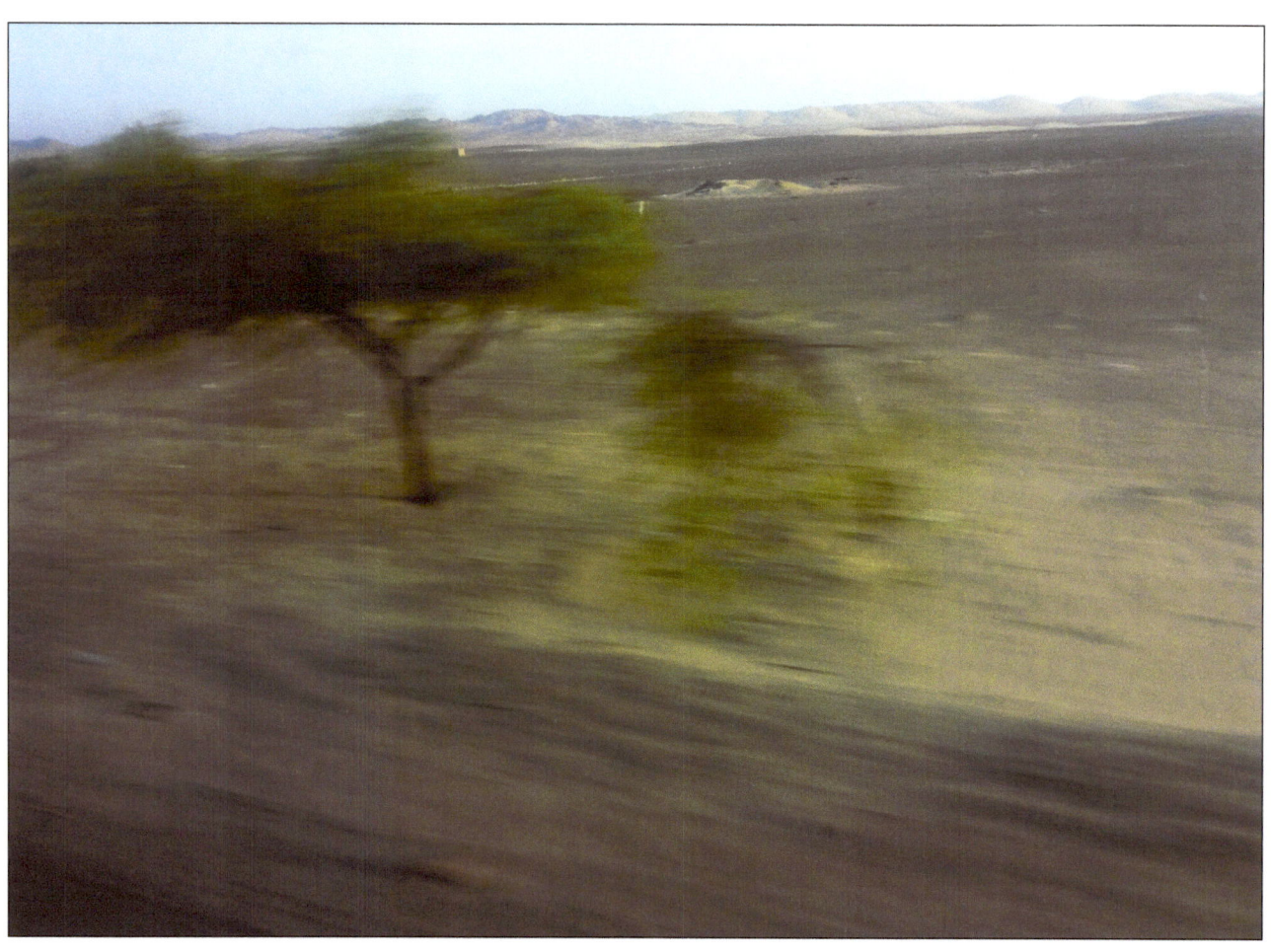

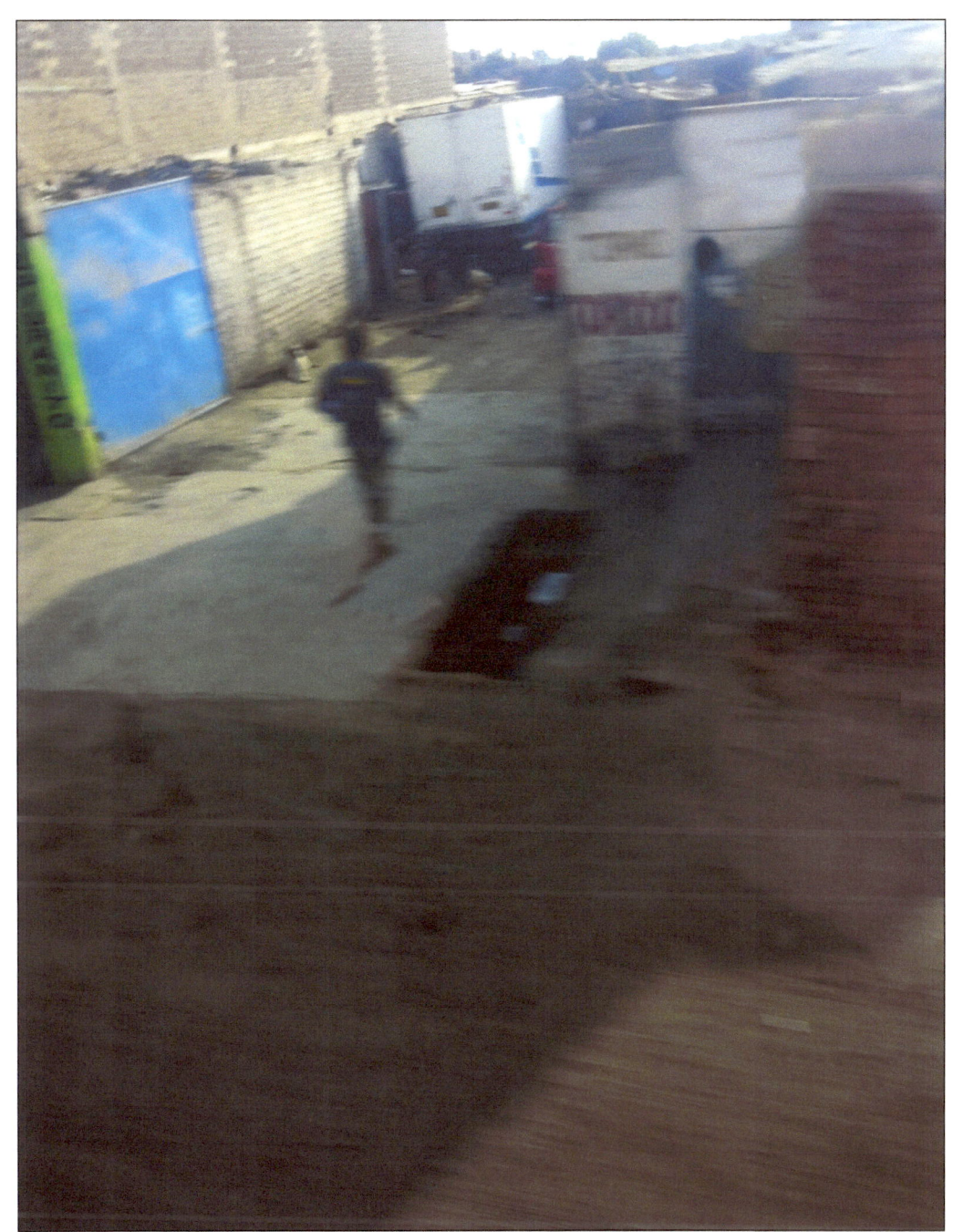

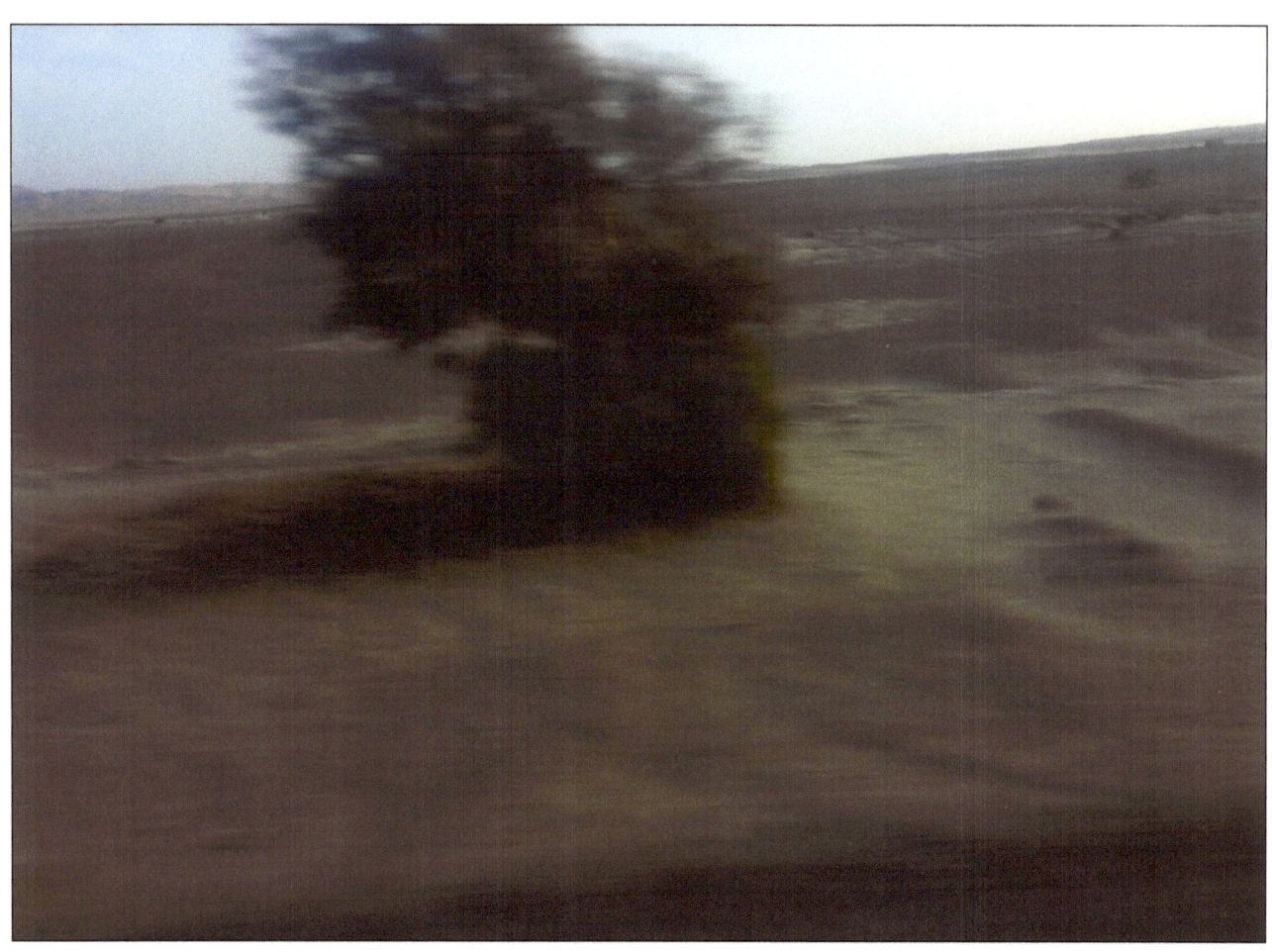

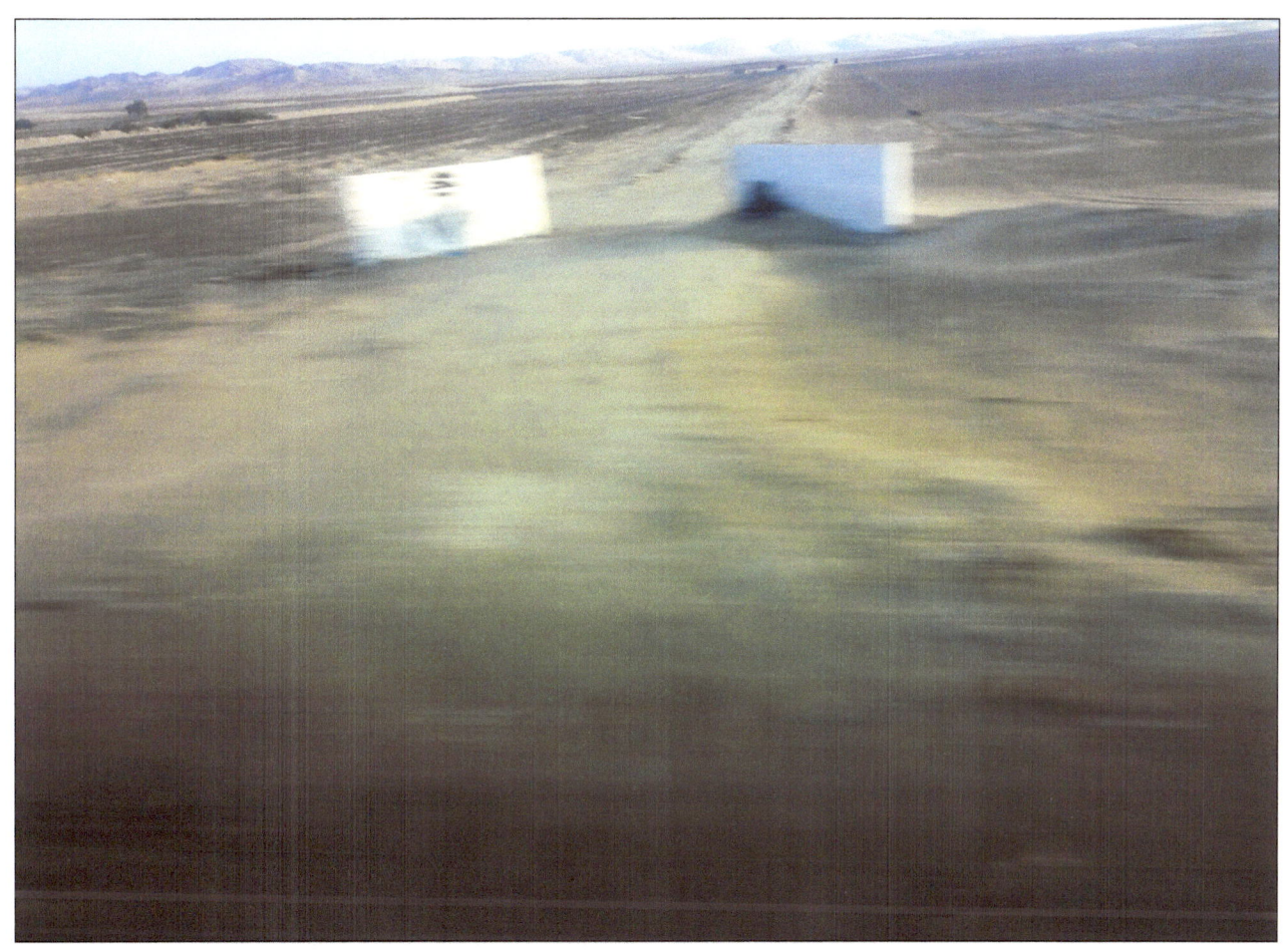

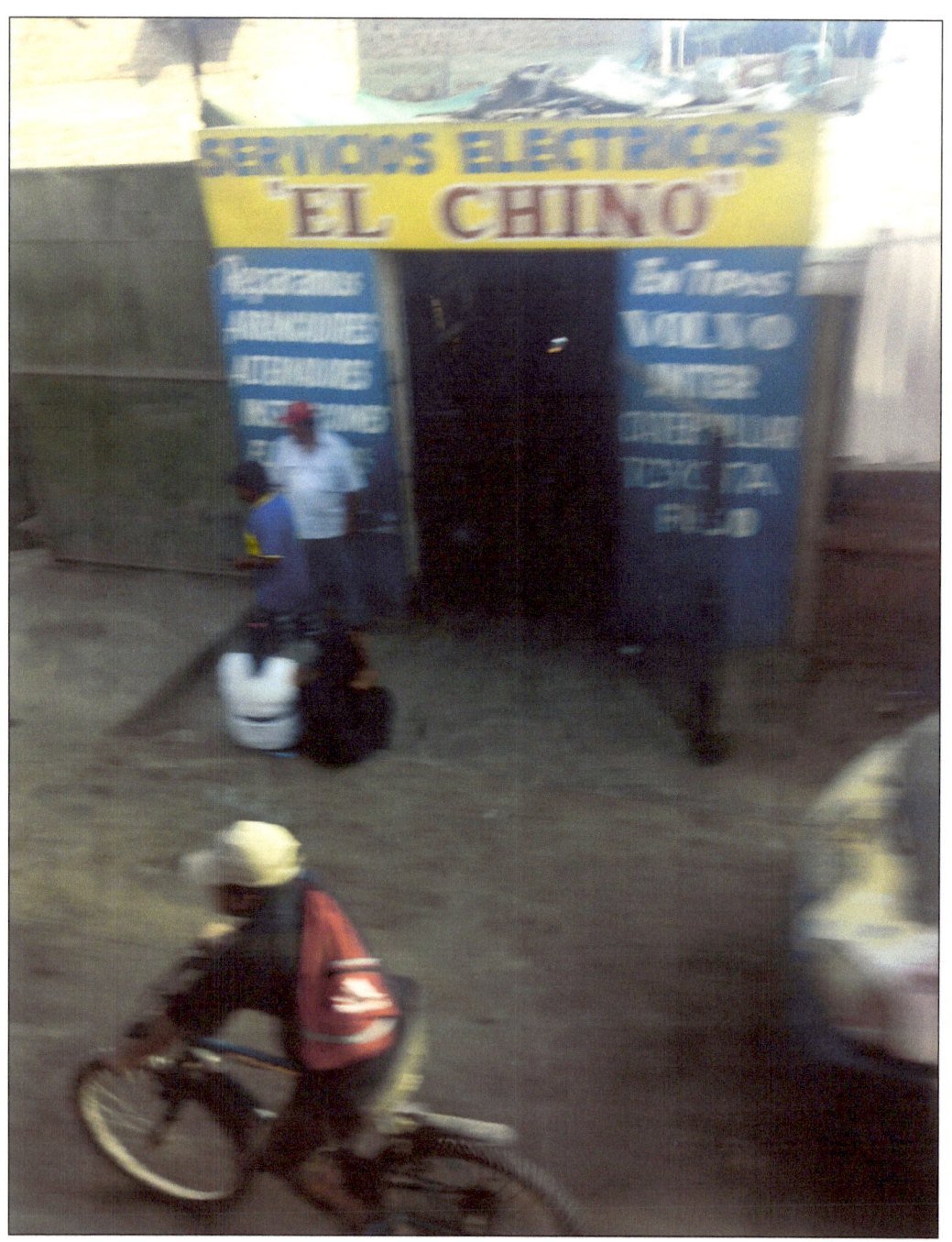

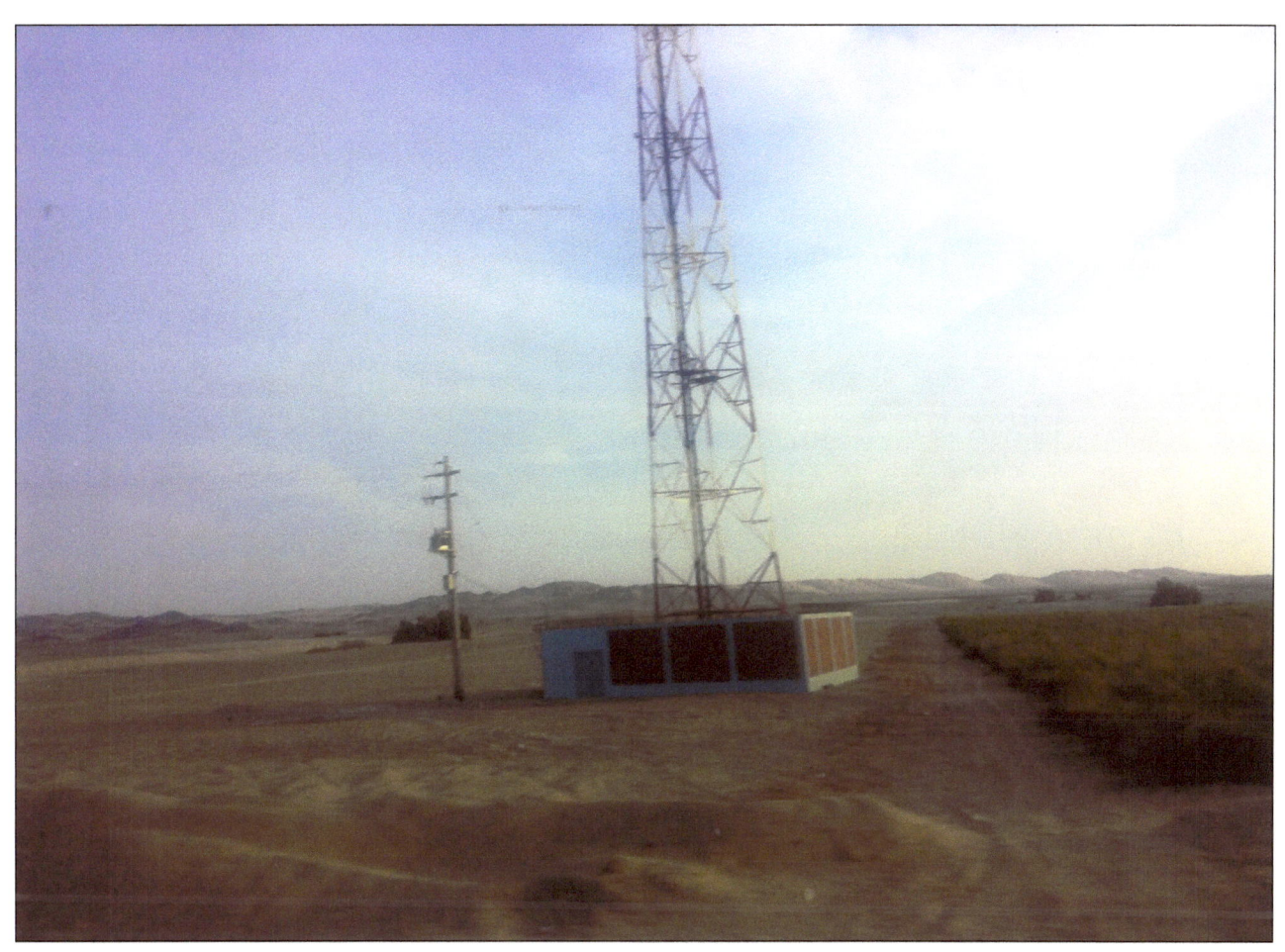

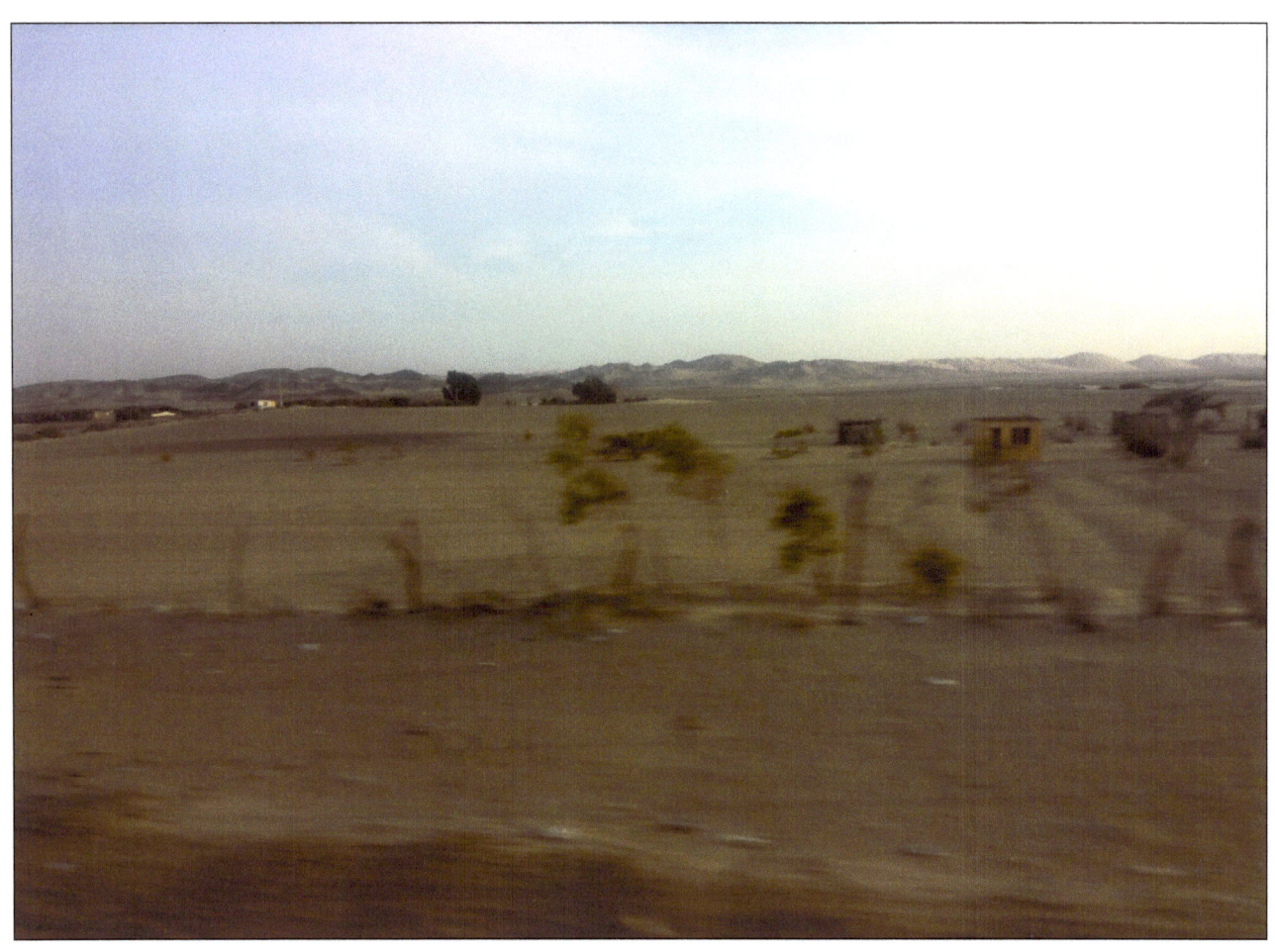

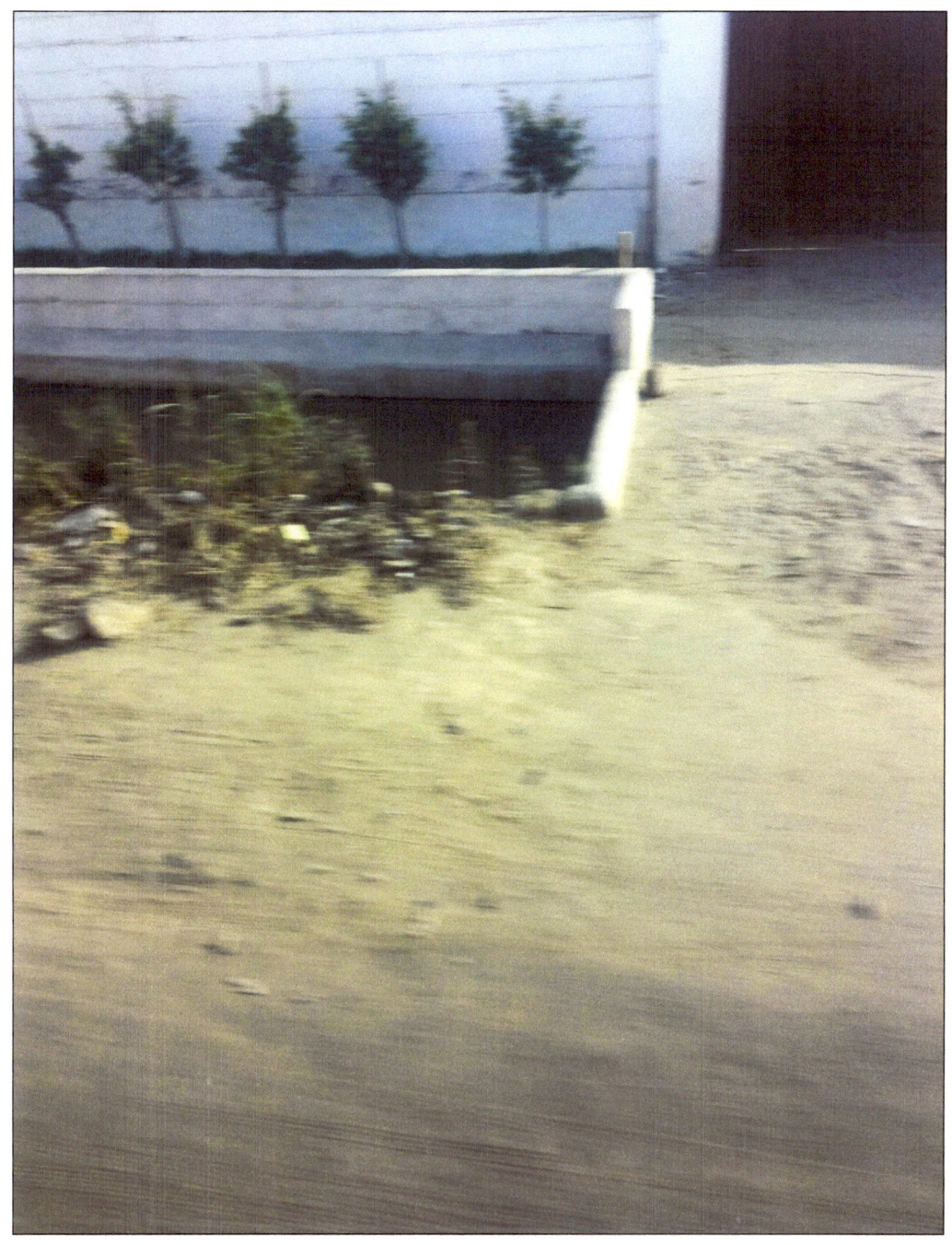

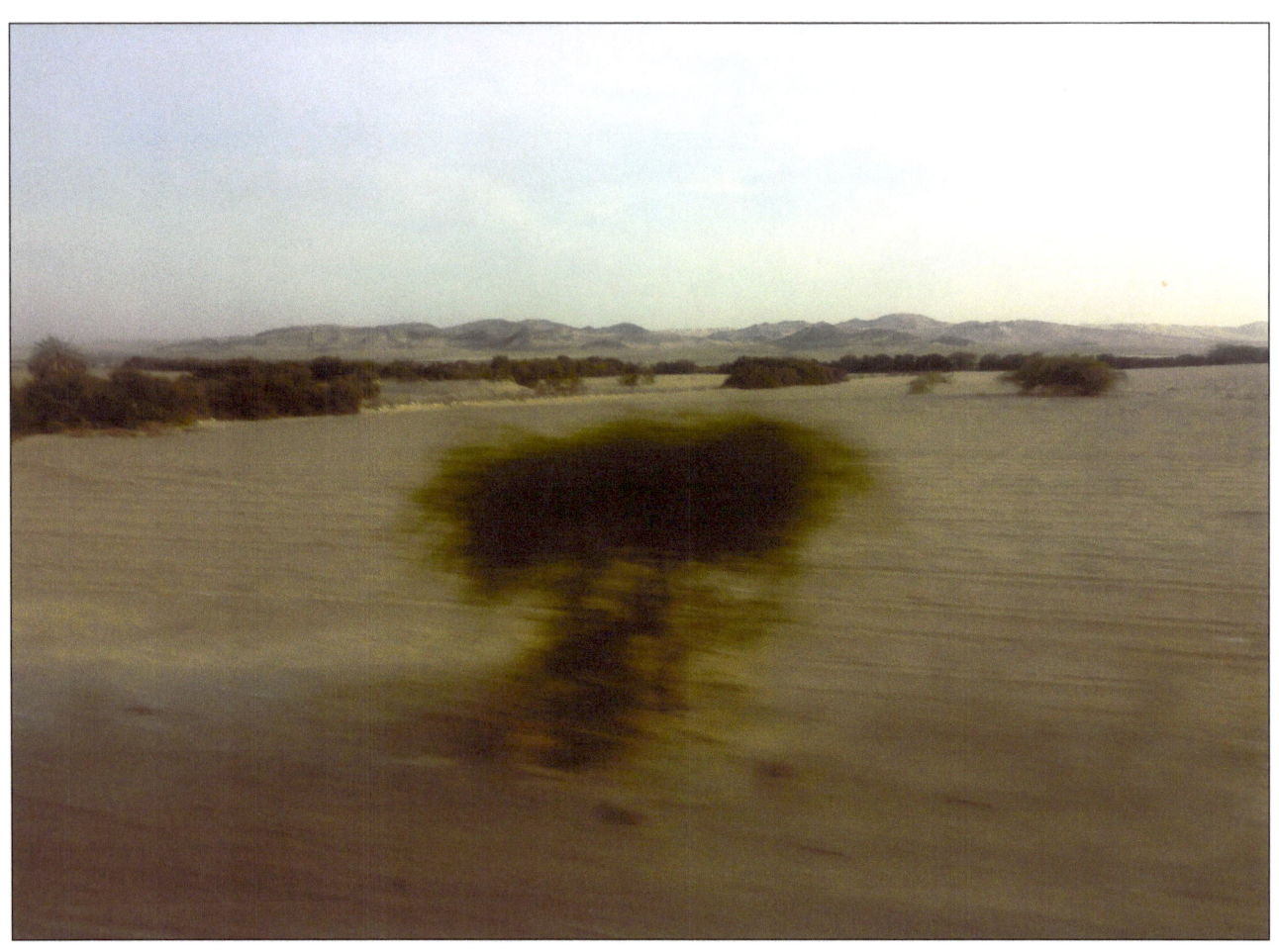

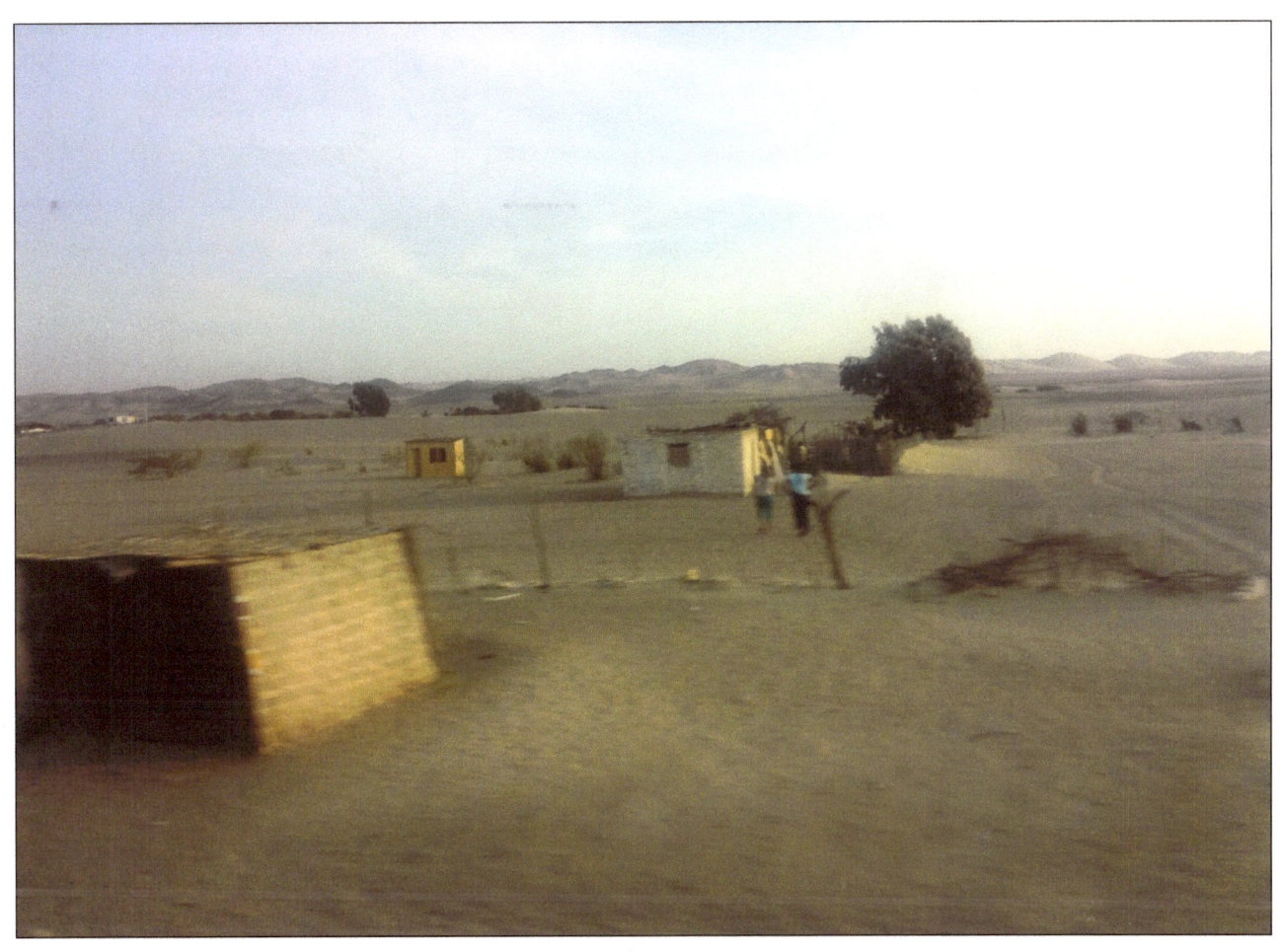

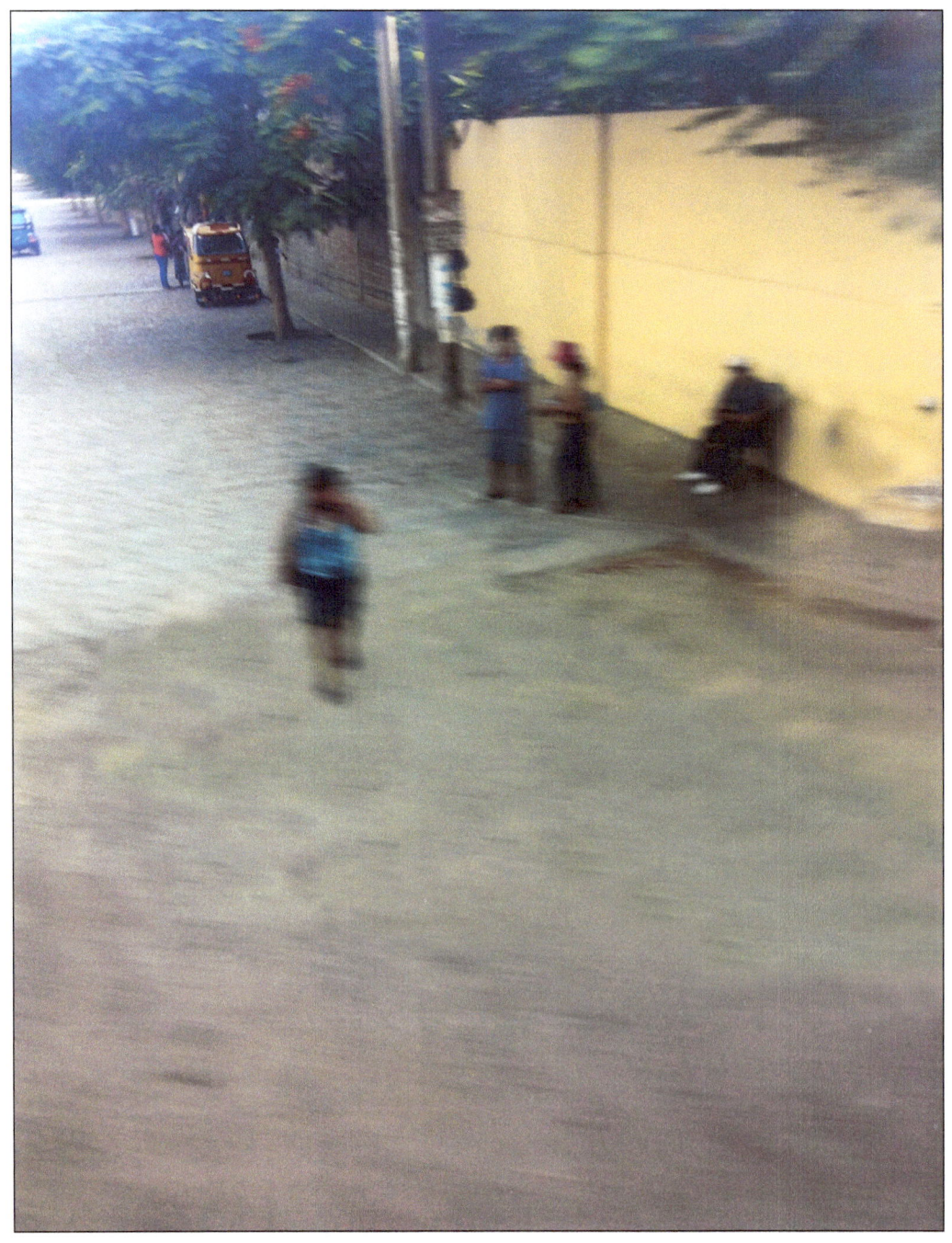

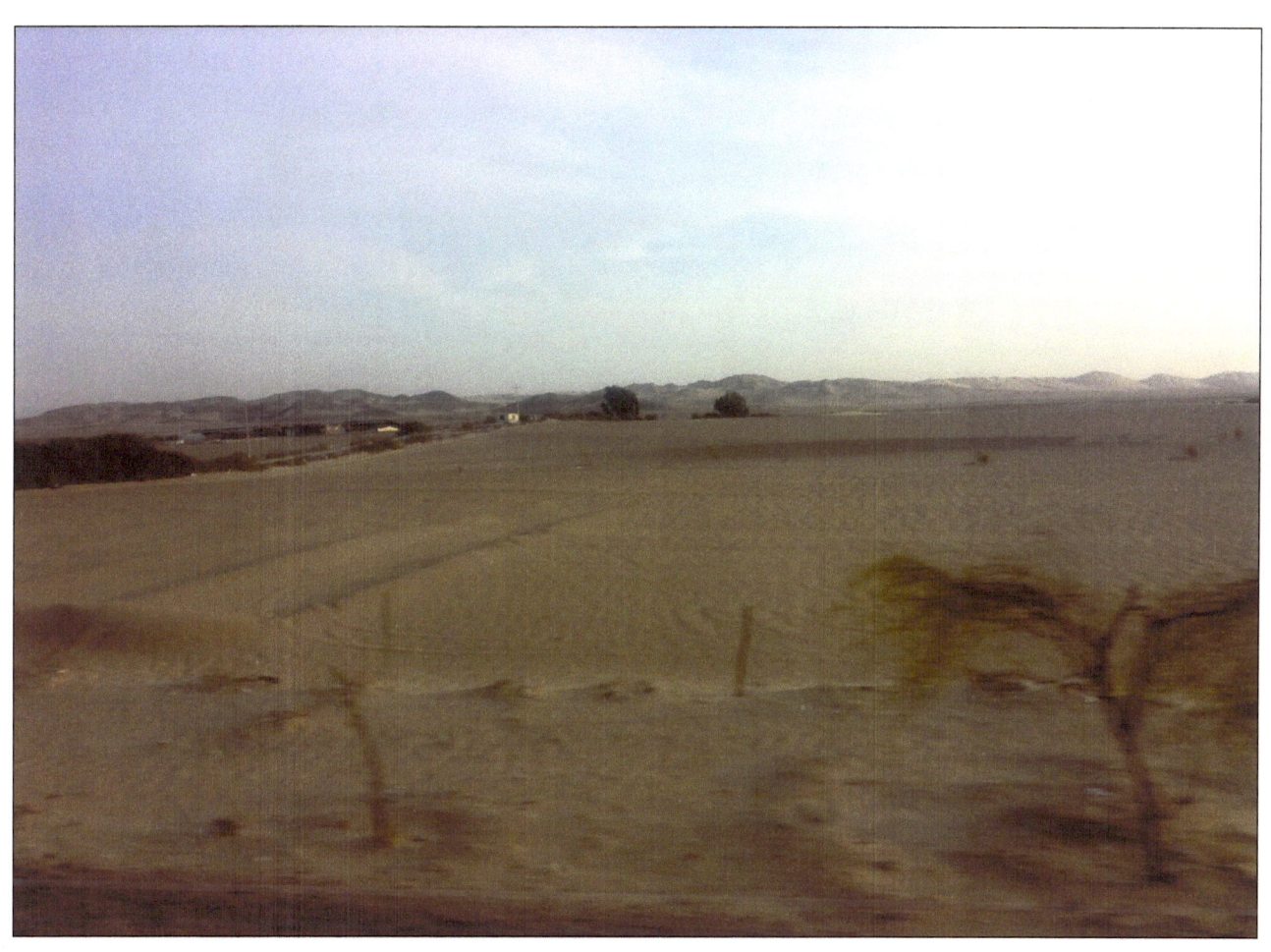

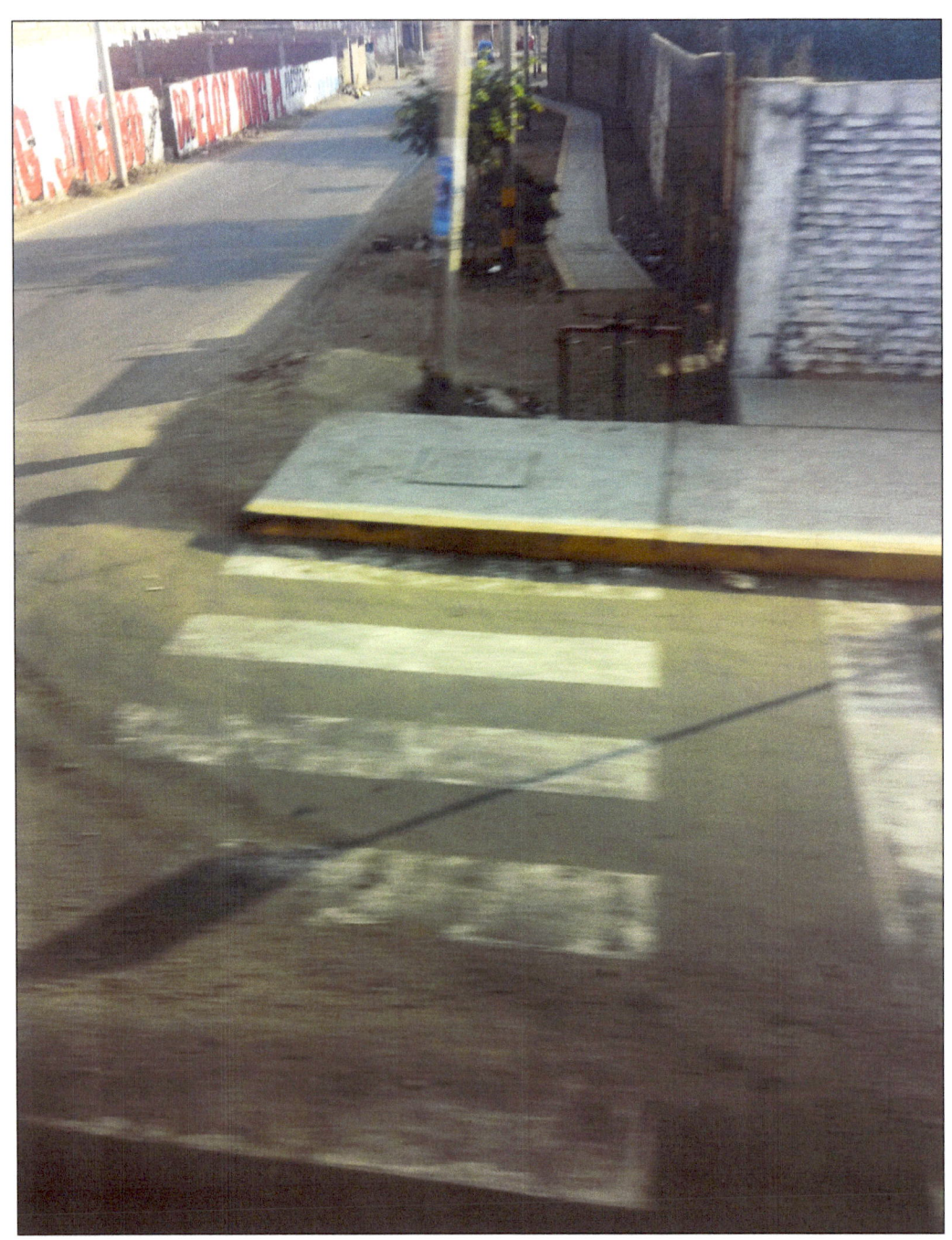

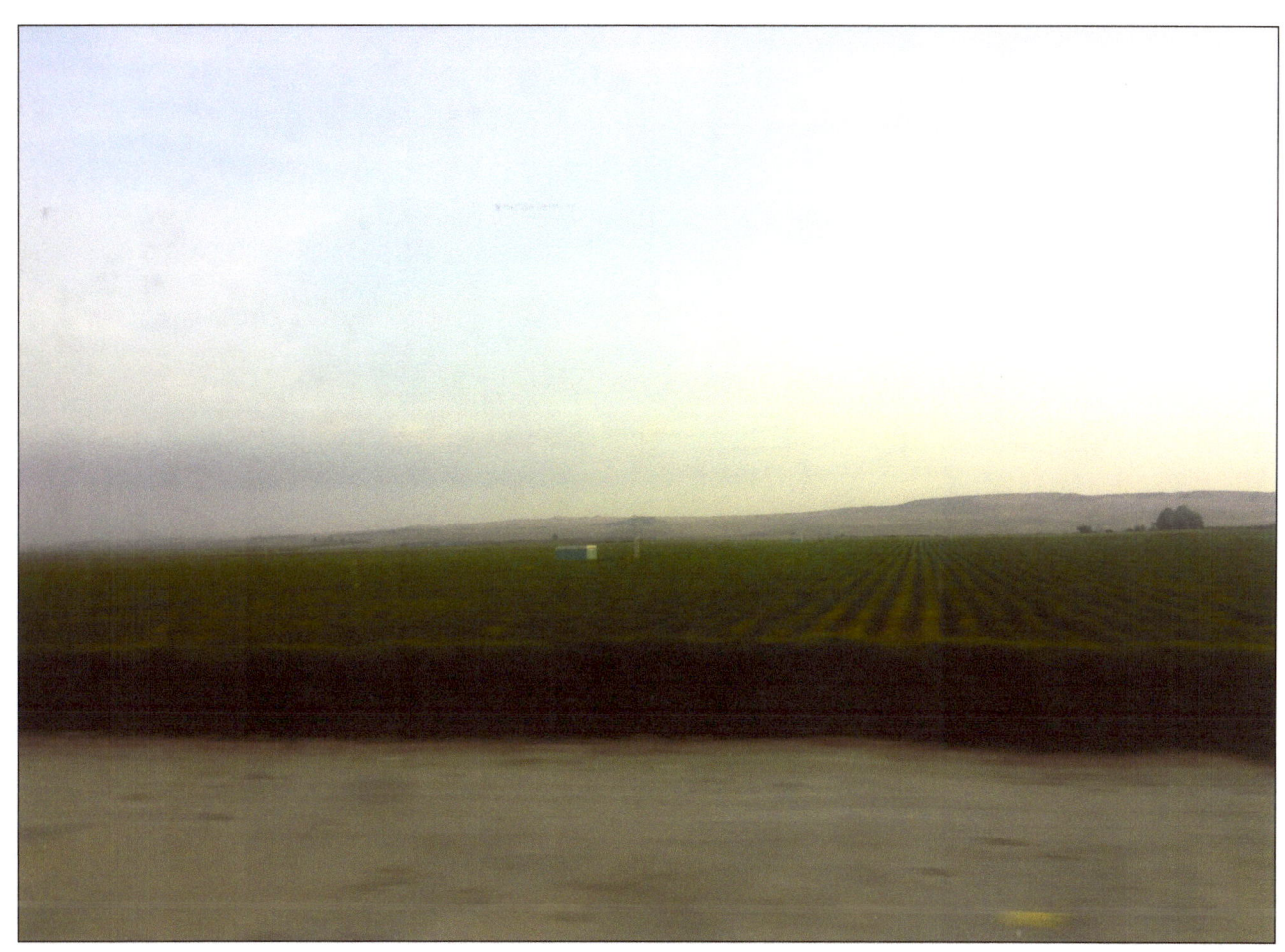

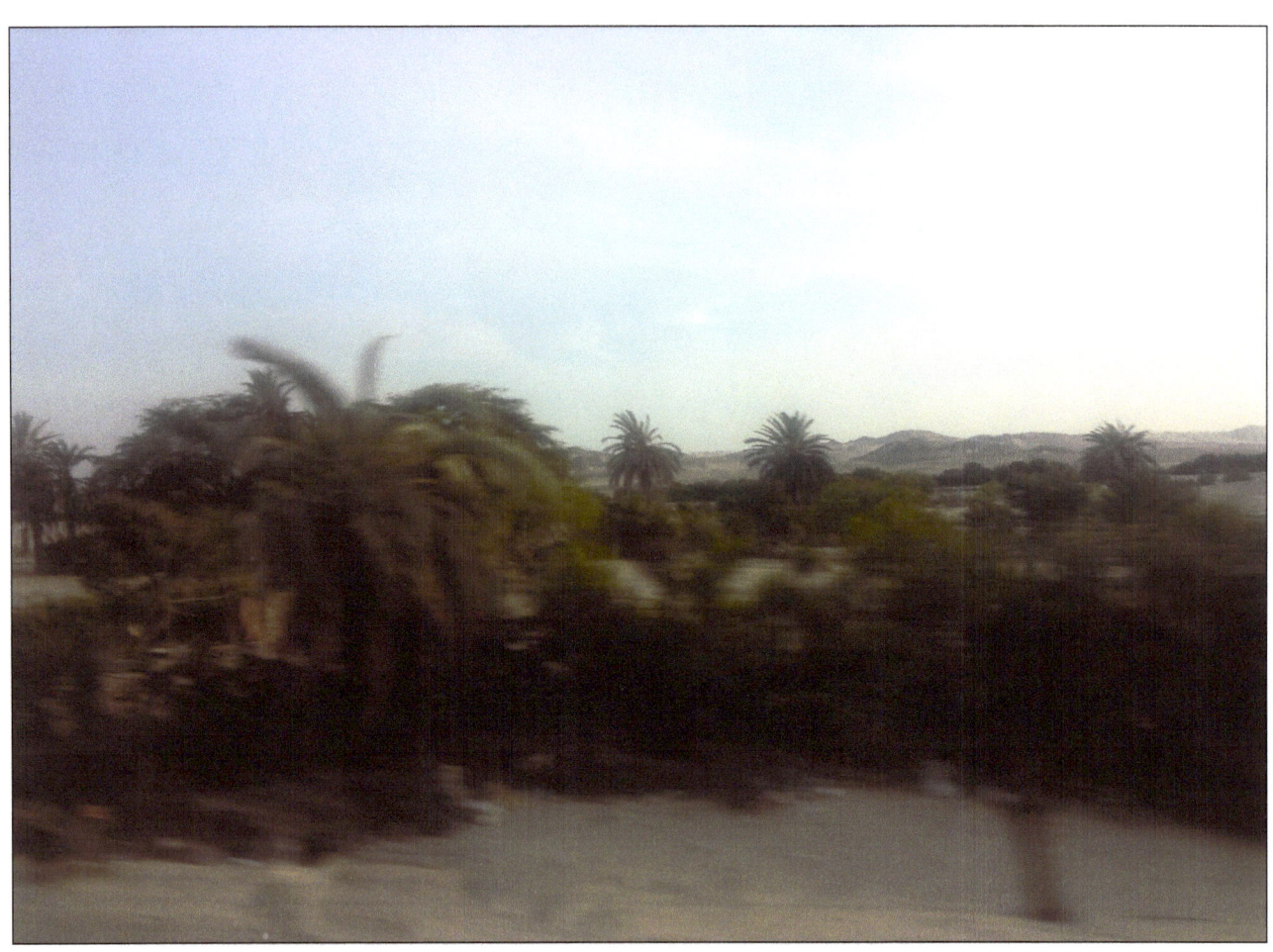

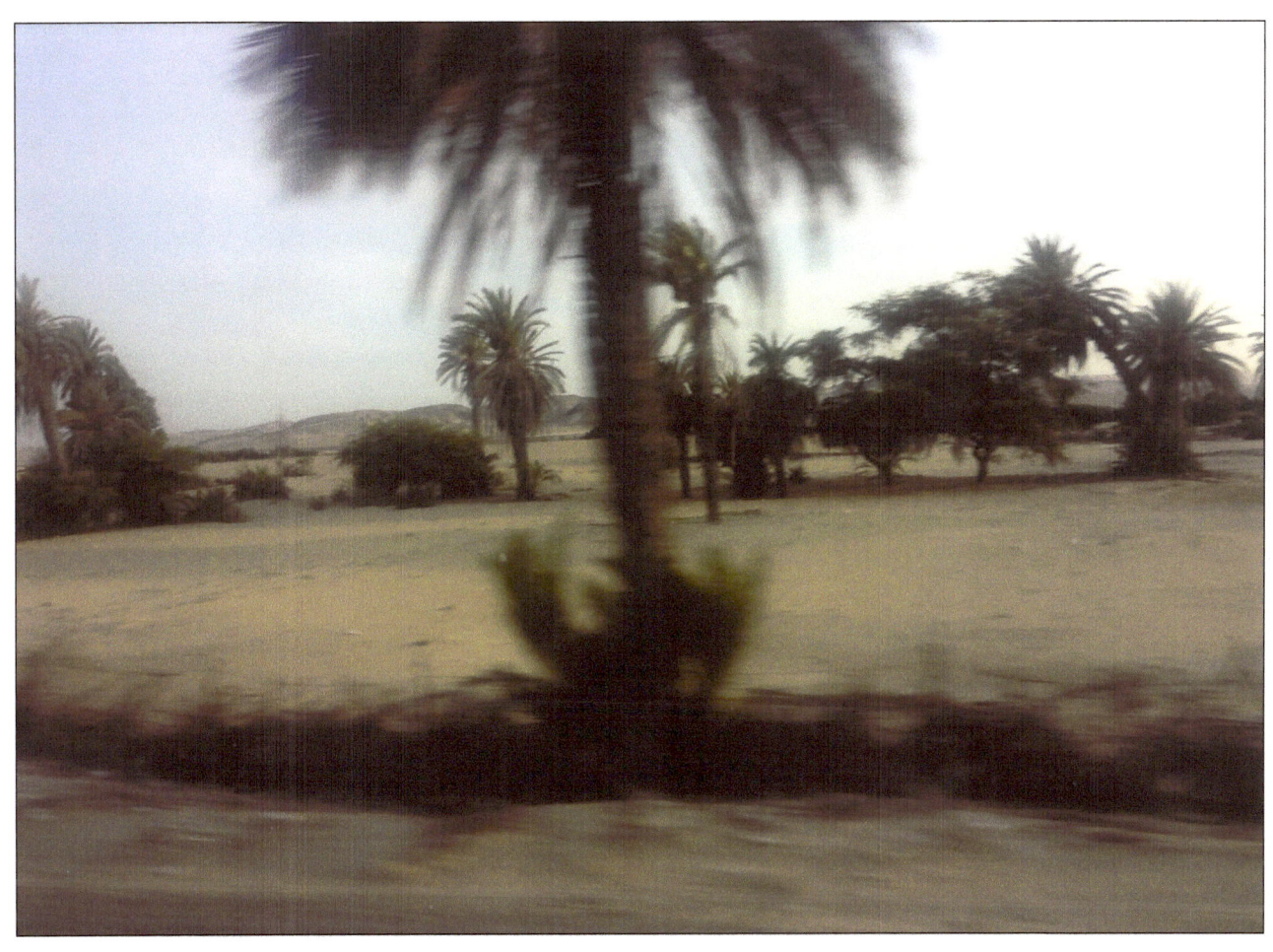

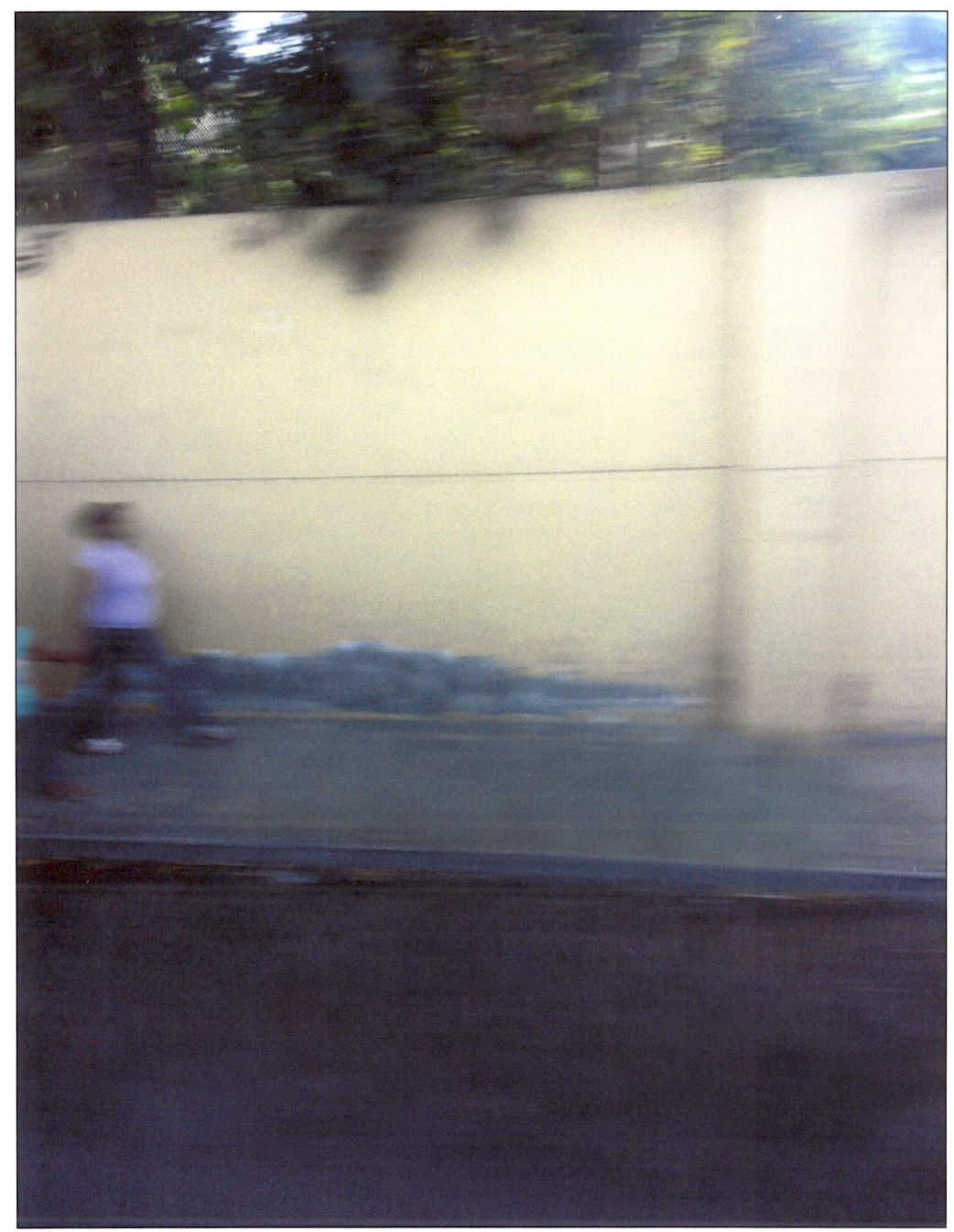

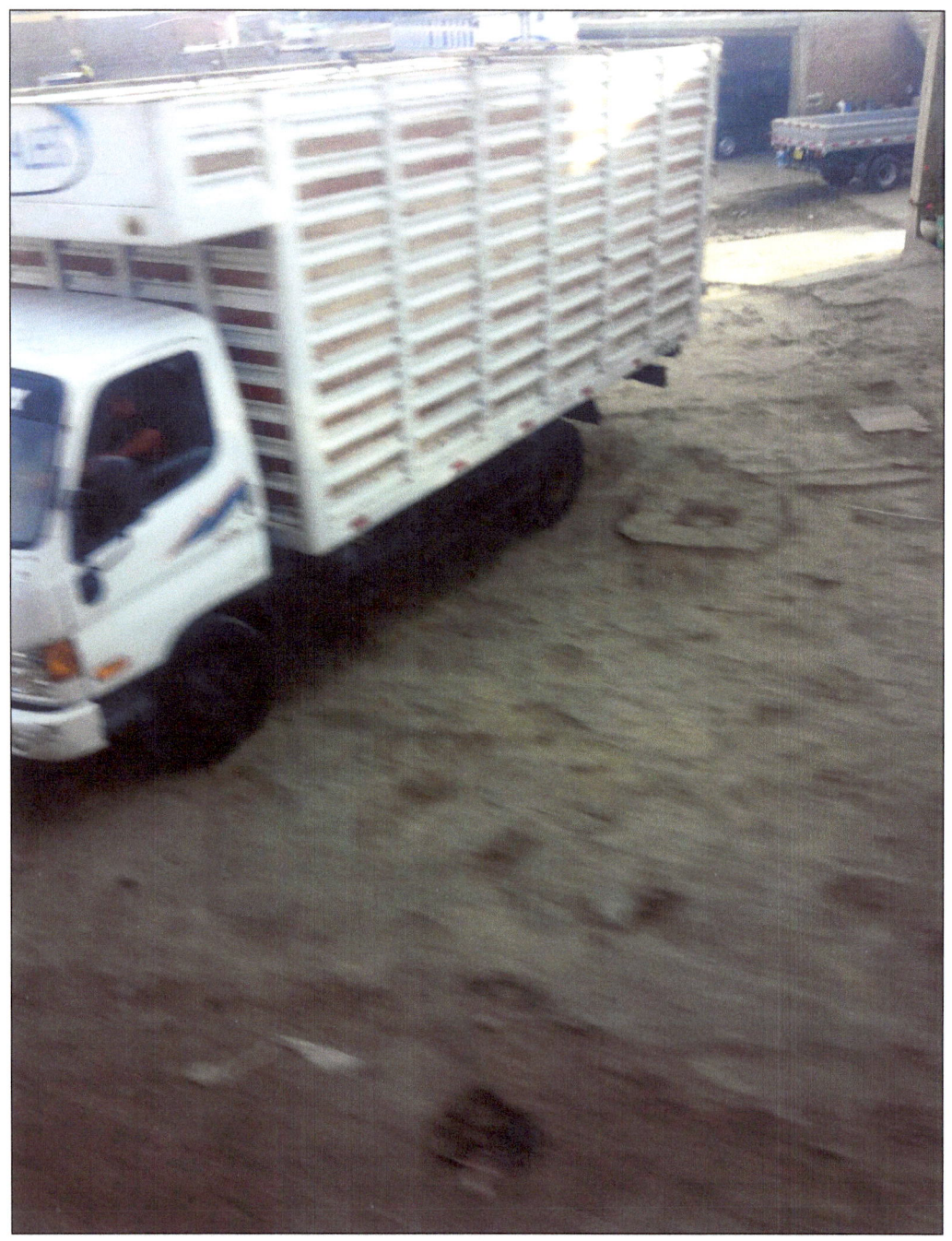

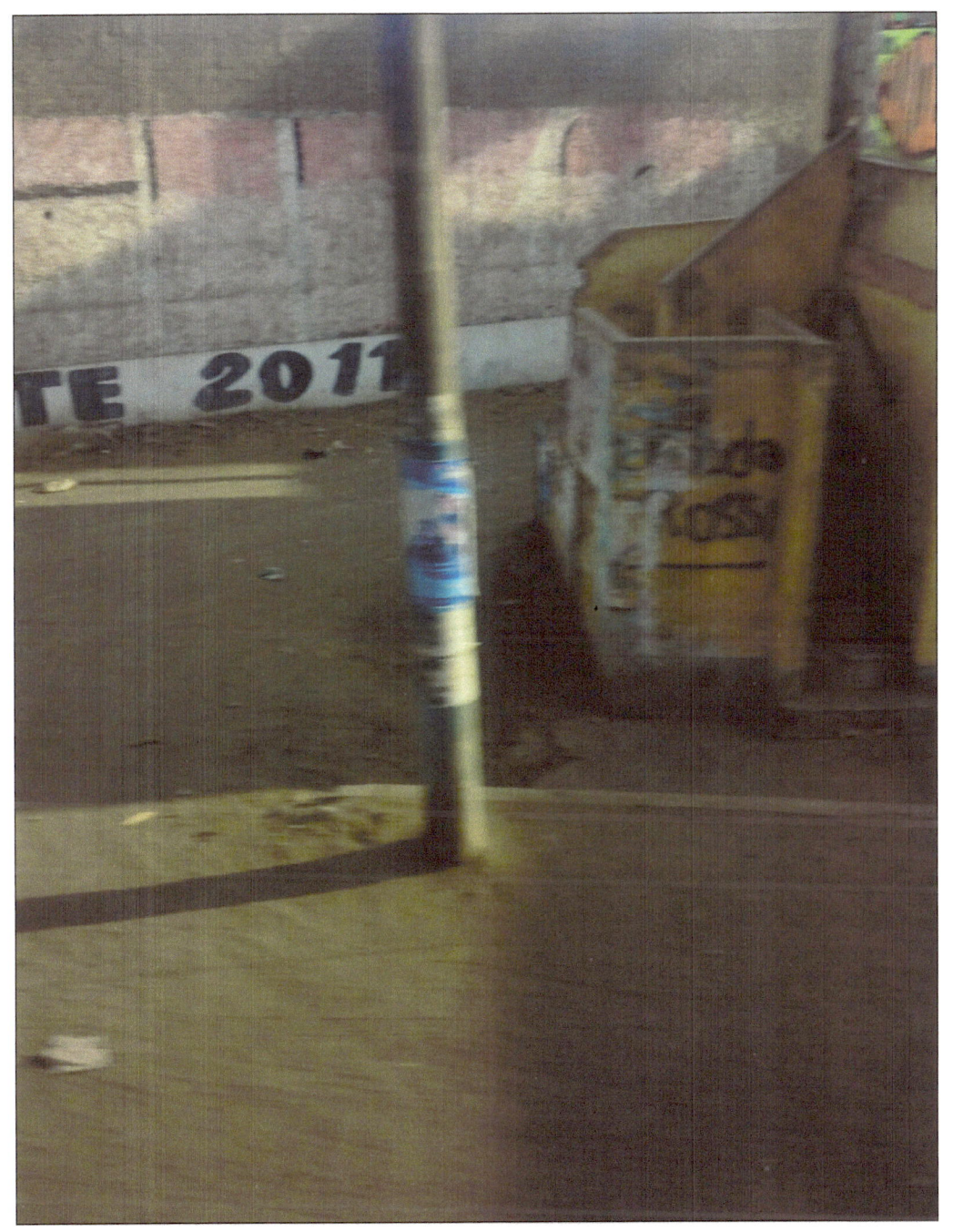

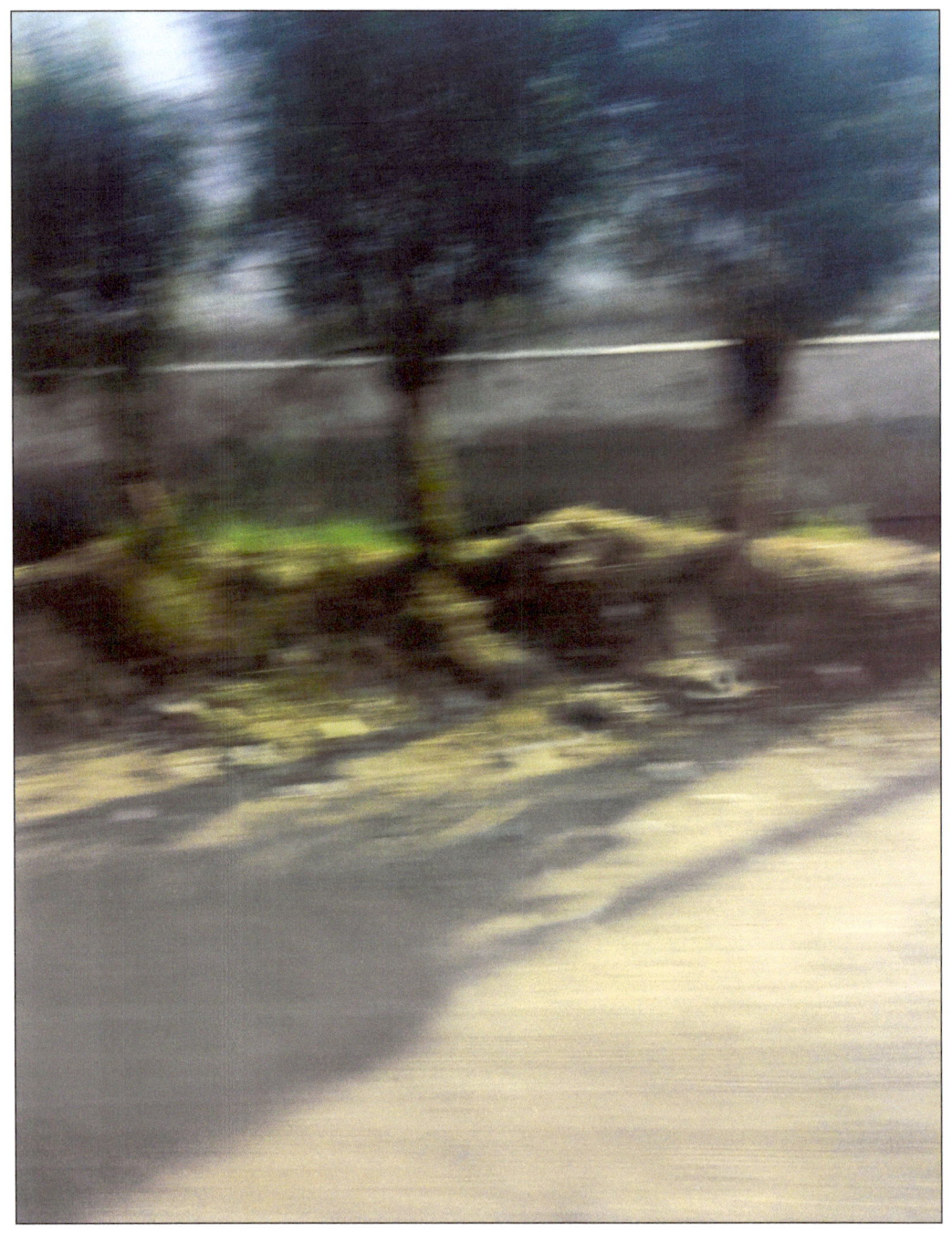

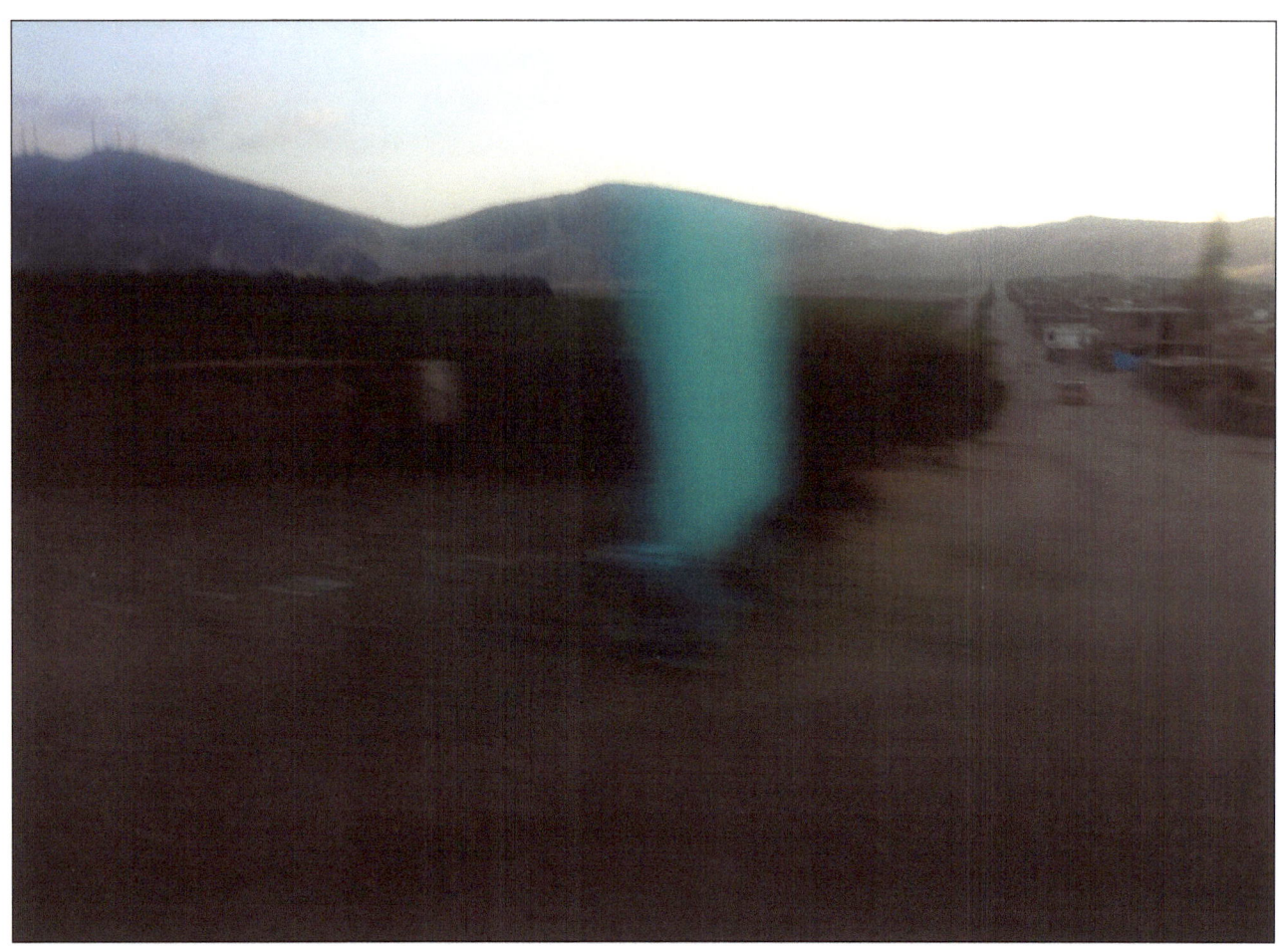

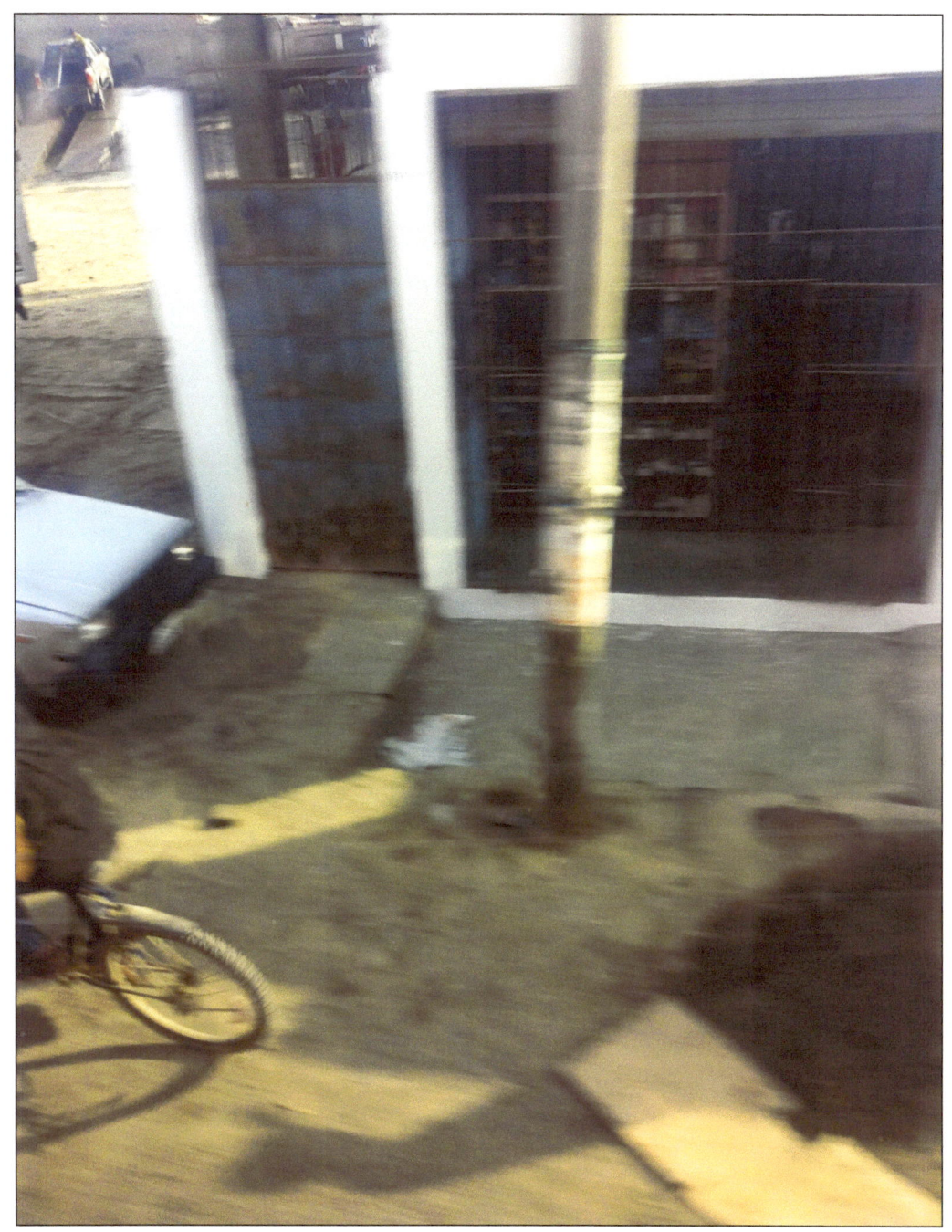

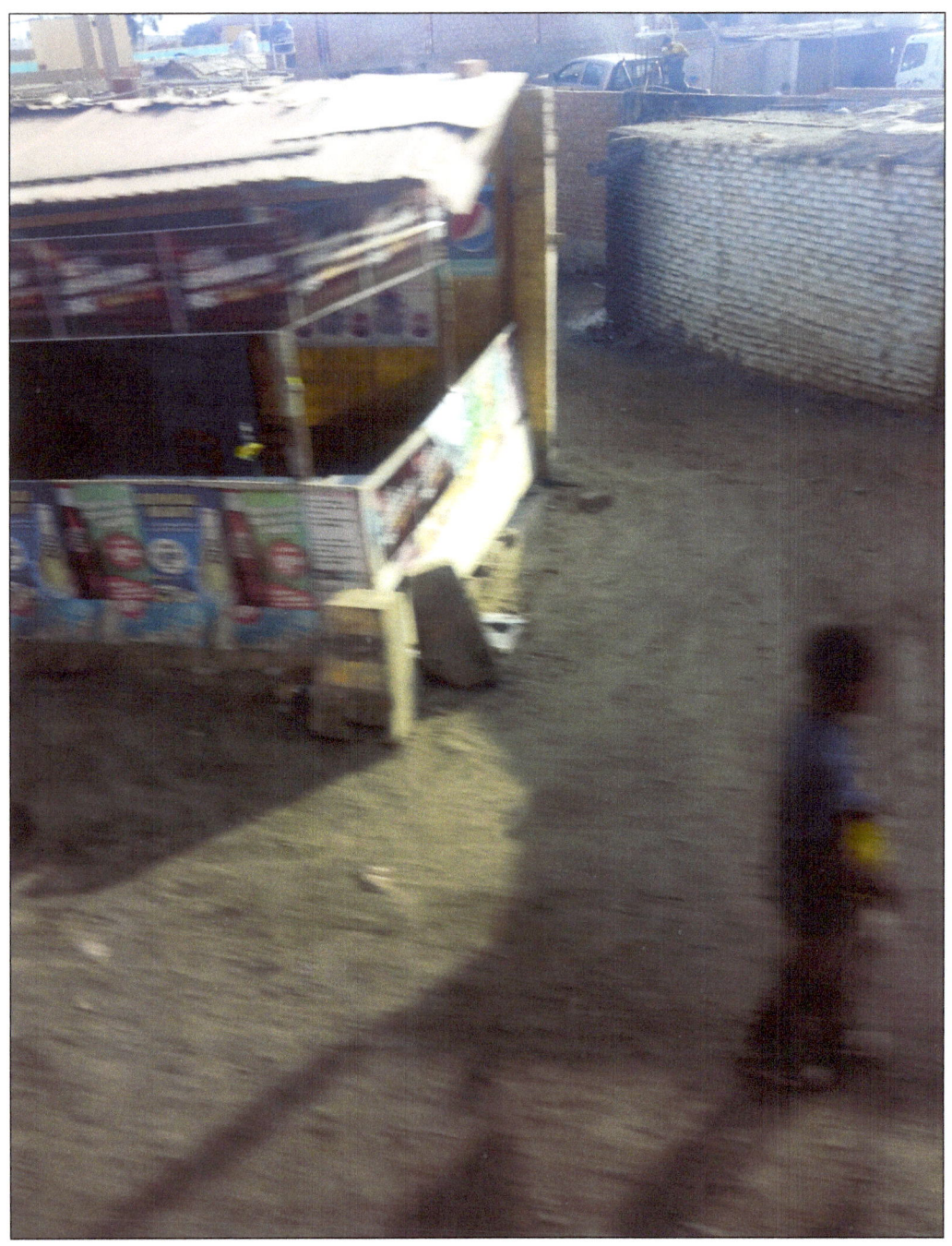

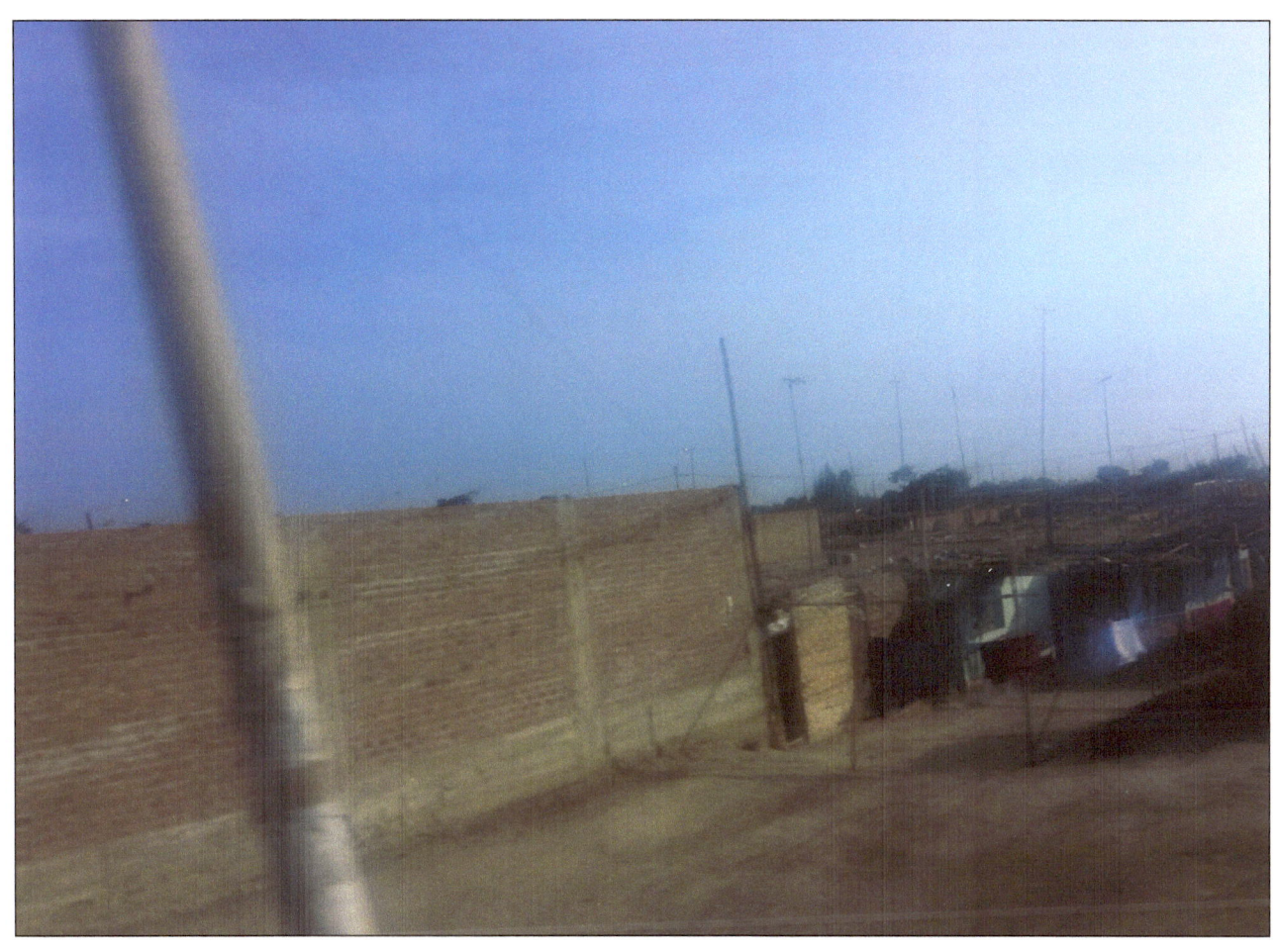

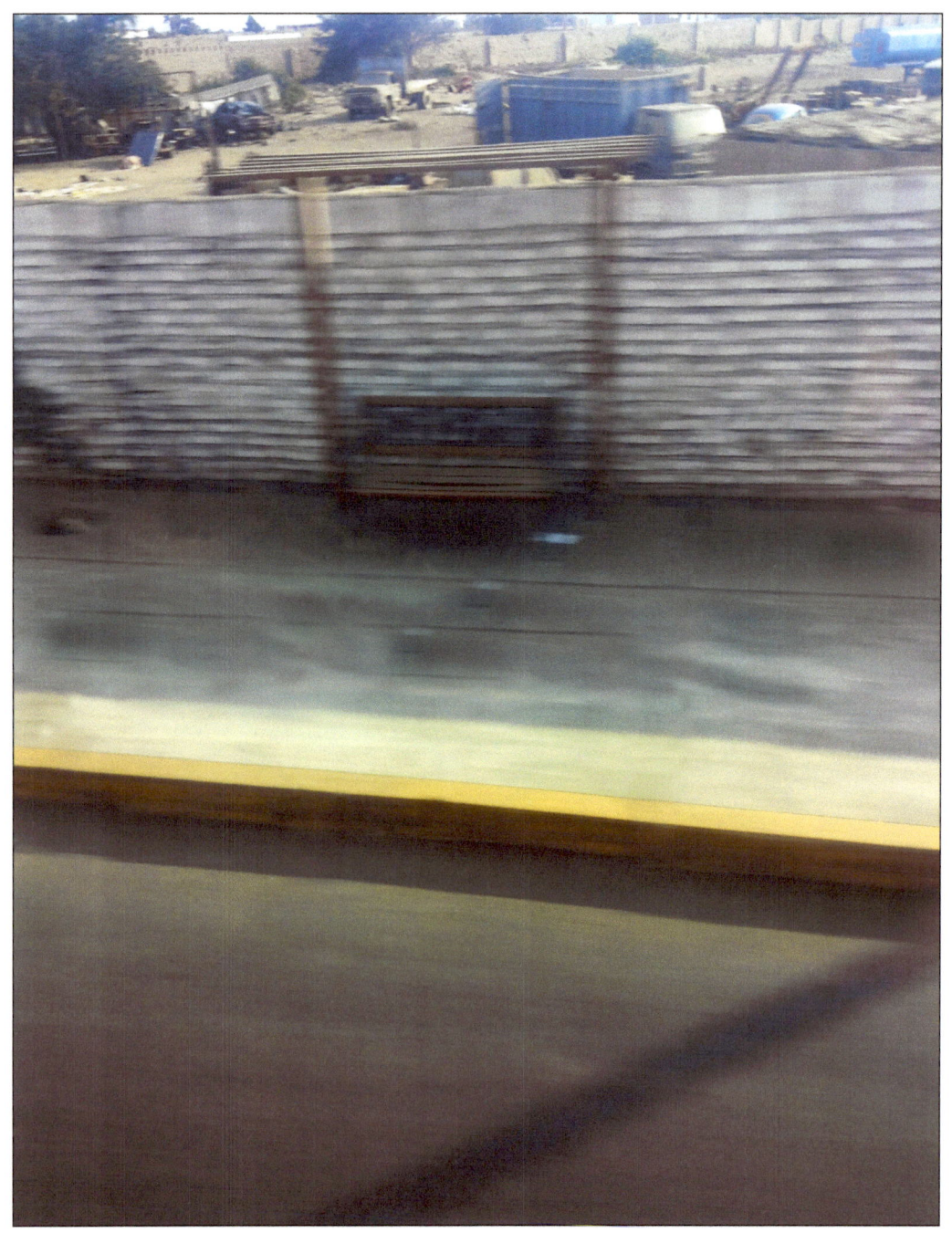

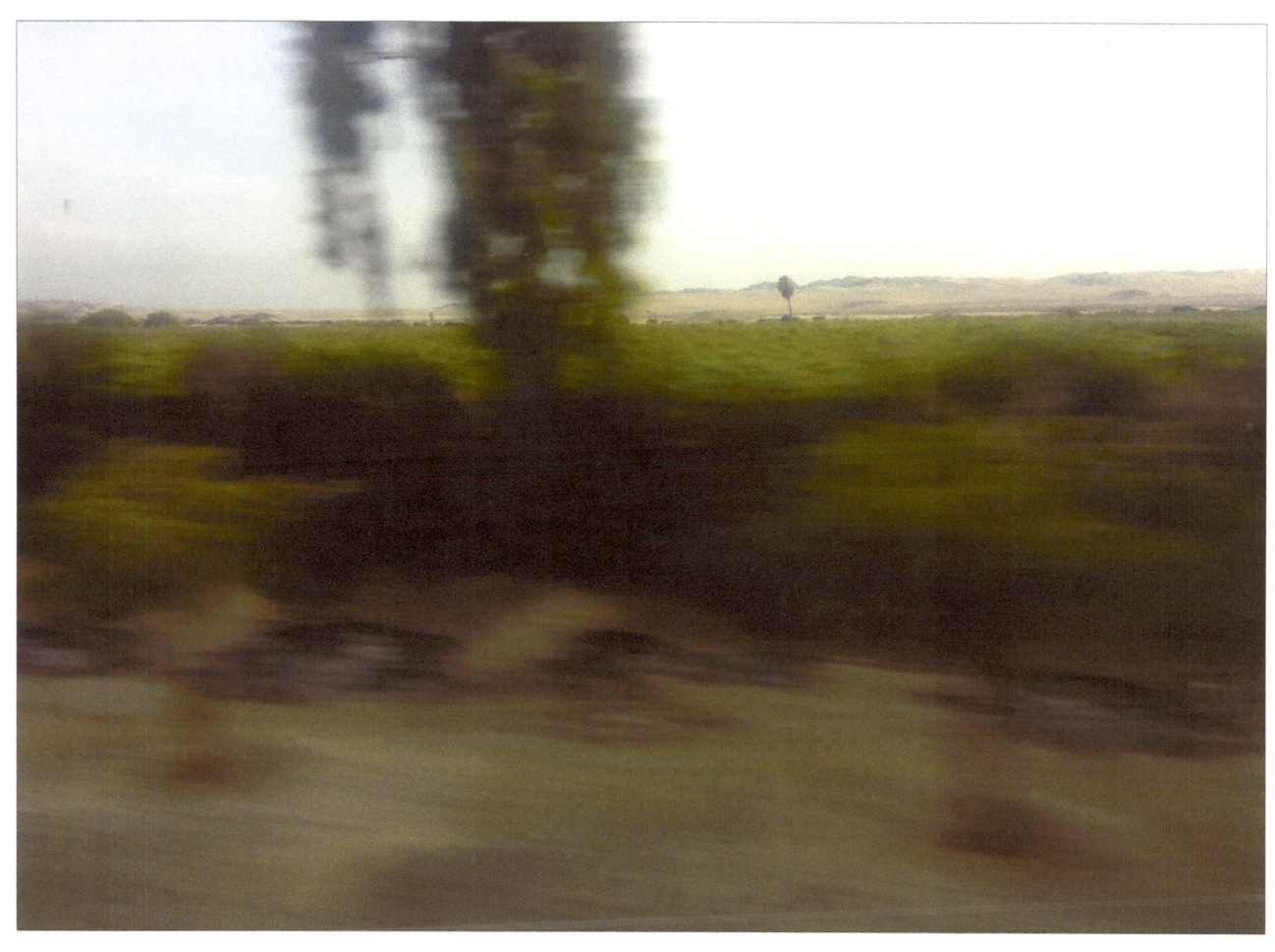

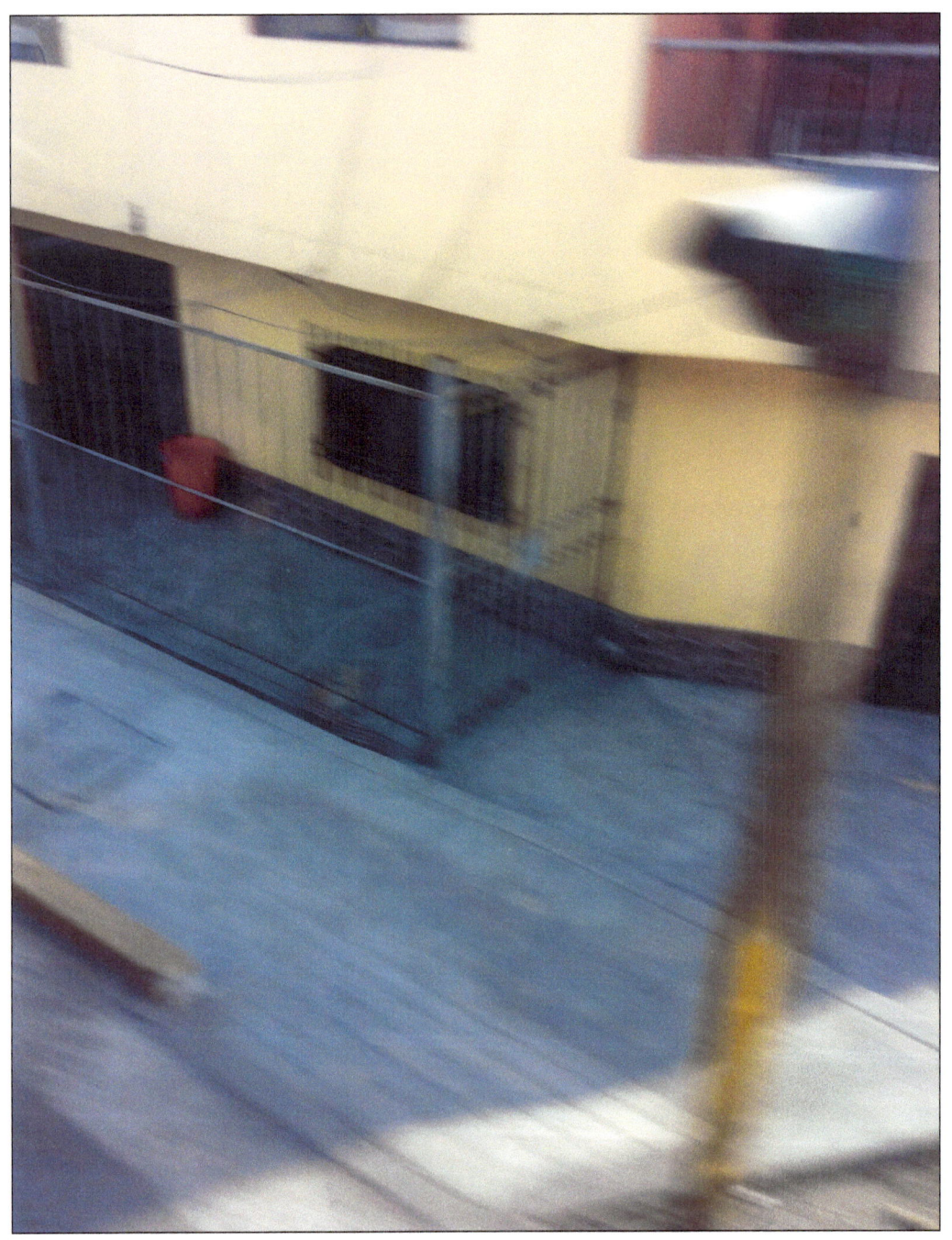

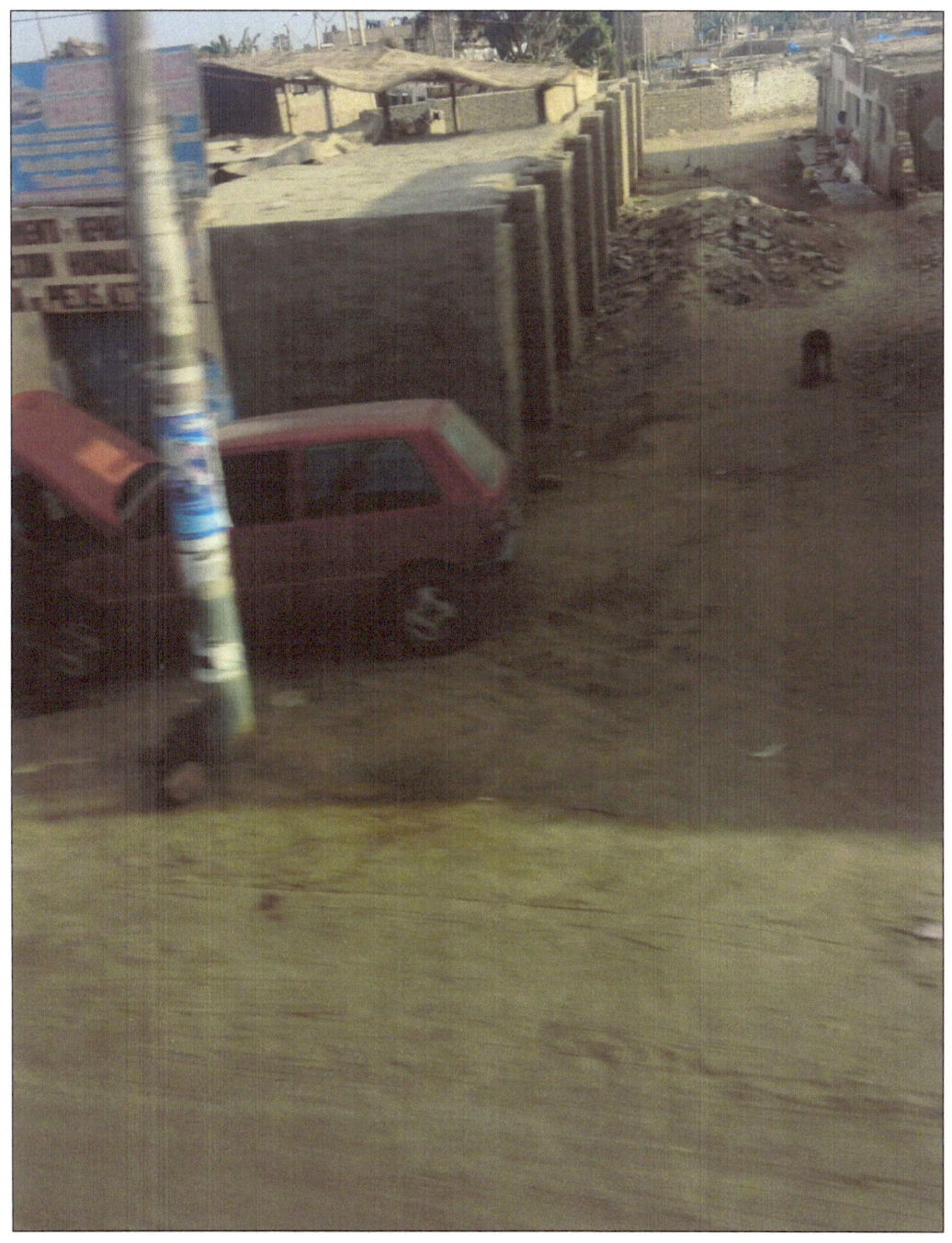

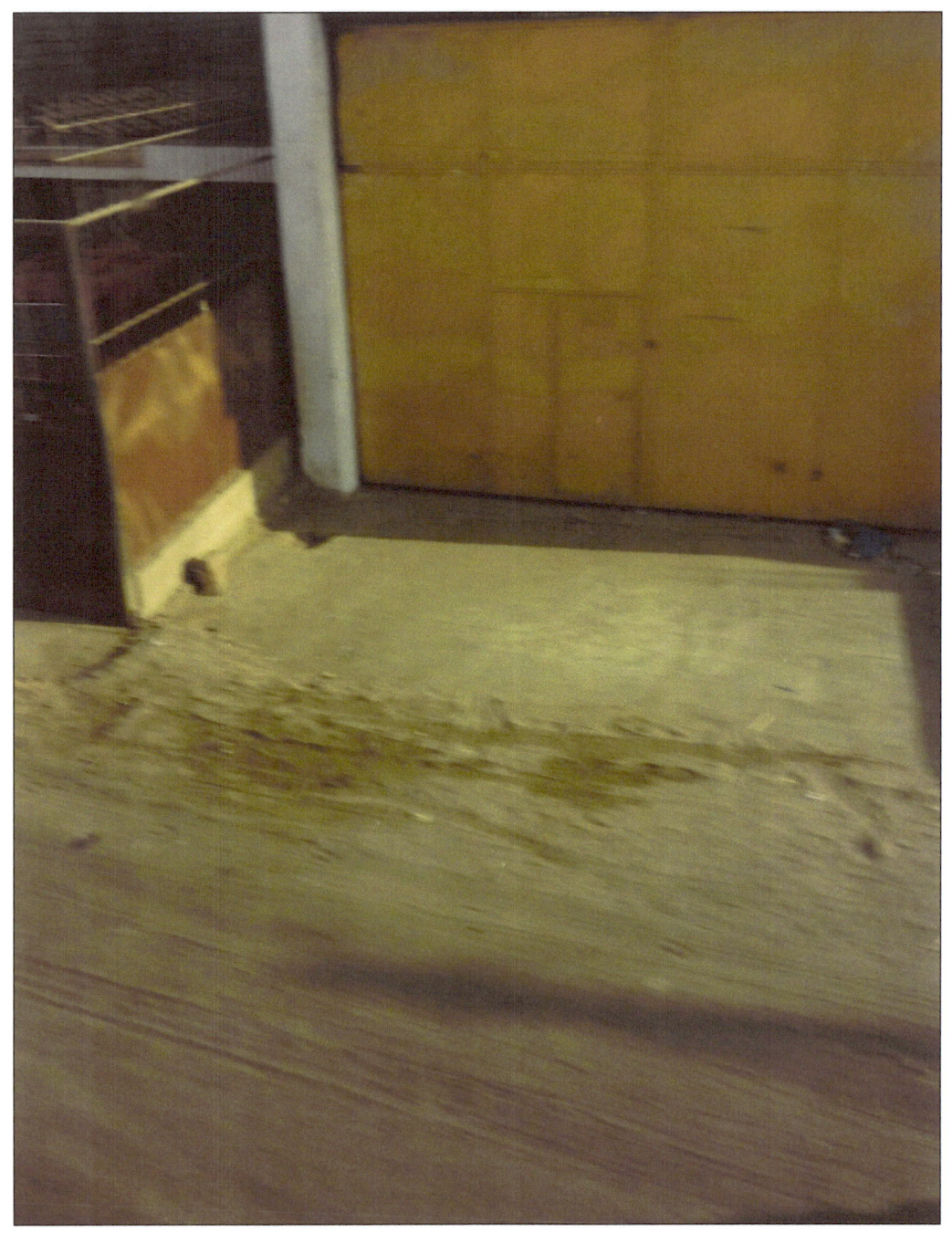

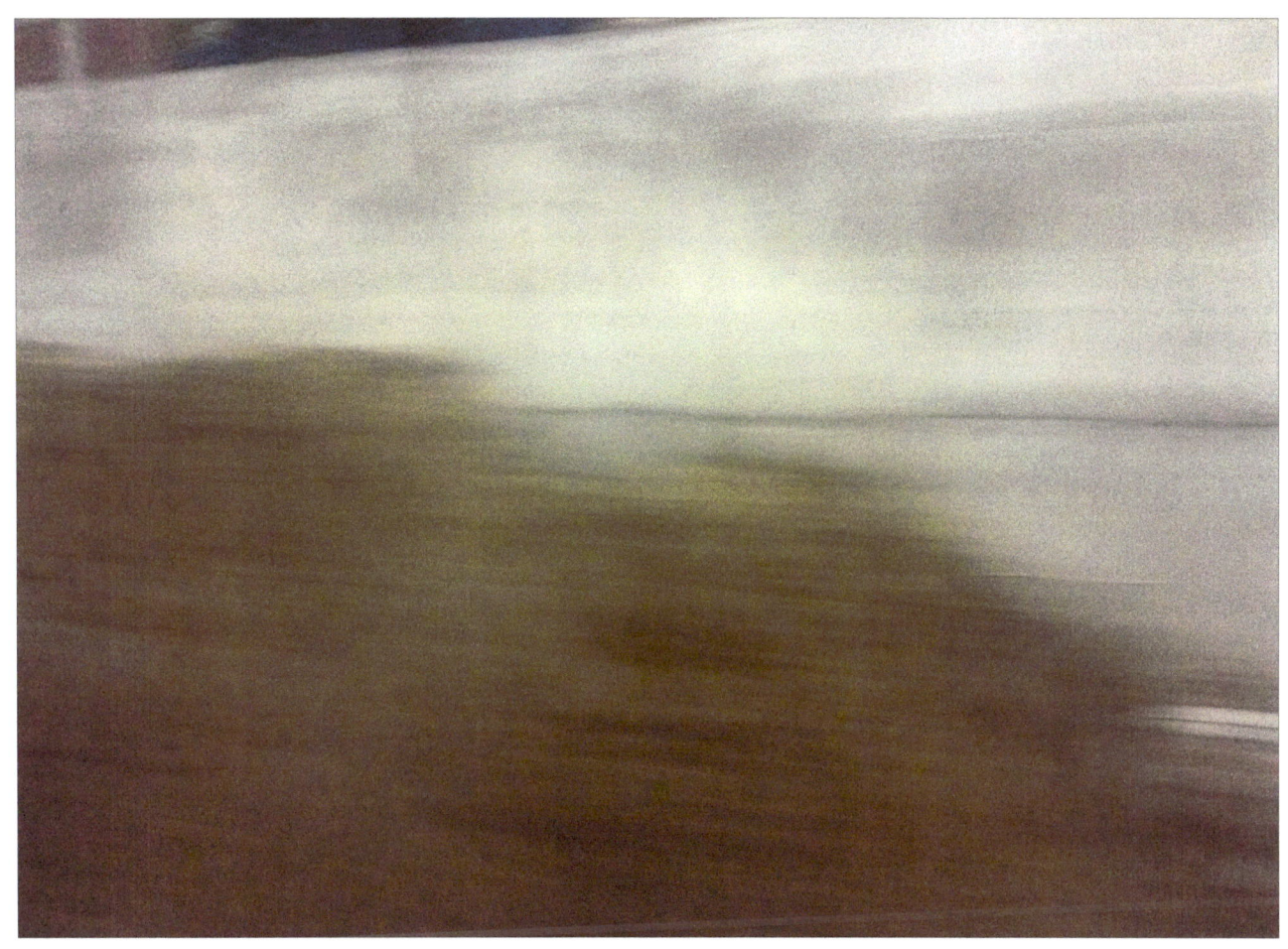

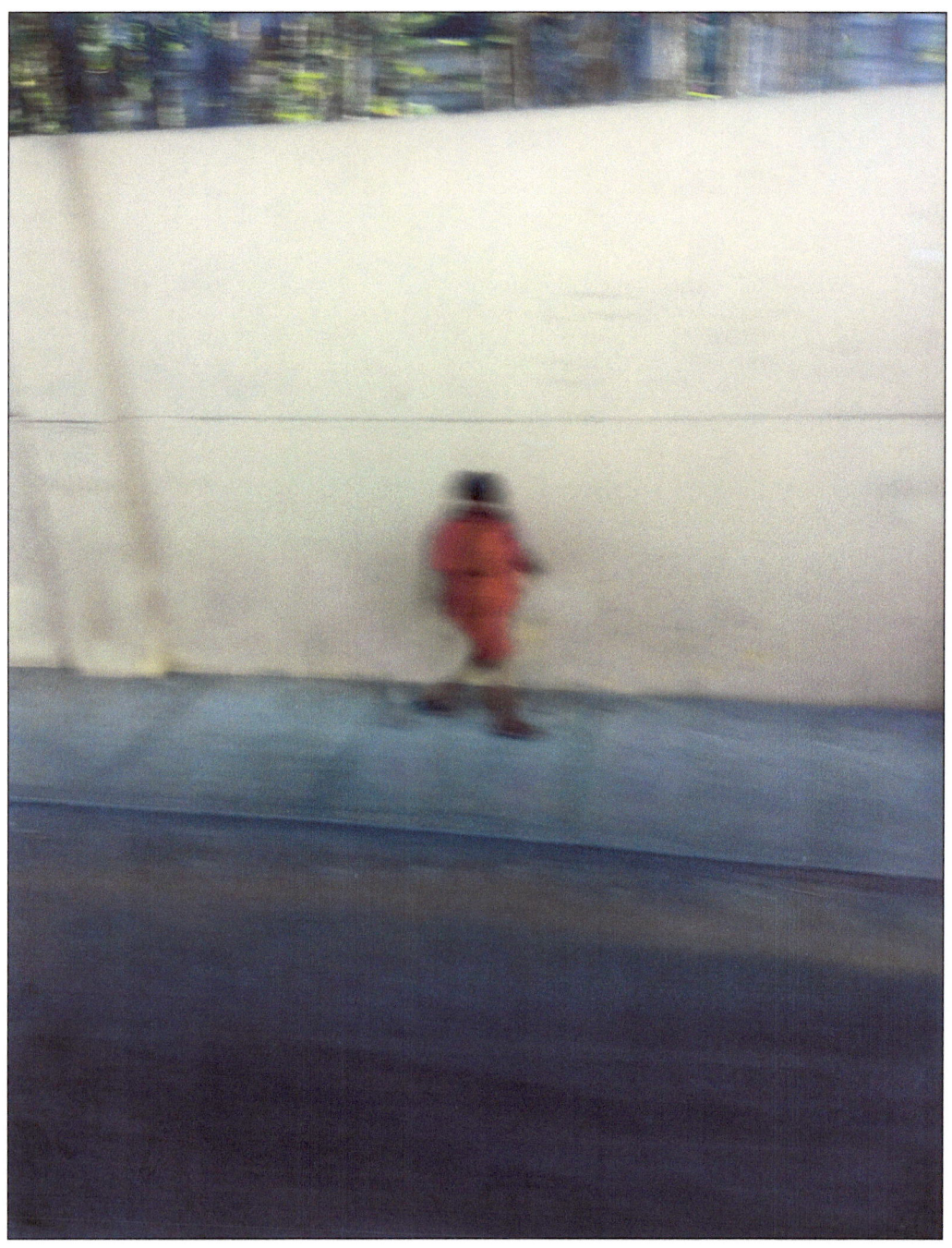

www.ingramcontent.com/pod-product-compliance
Lightning Source LLC
Chambersburg PA
CBHW051218220526
45473CB00003B/1089